the **VAN DIEMEN**
ANTHOLOGY 2019

THE VAN DIEMEN HISTORY PRIZE

Writing and history have long been lovers, both needing and complementing each other. Non-fiction can make for compelling reading, no matter what the subject, and this is arguably truest when the subject is history. One has only to look at the books – and the sales figures – of Dava Sobel about longitude and Simon Singh about mathematics to see that the work of historians and the art of good writing are natural partners.

It is that collaboration, that love affair, that The Van Diemen History Prize celebrates.

—Chris Champion,
Editor, *Tasmania 40°South* magazine

the VAN DIEMEN ANTHOLOGY 2019

the best of
the VAN DIEMEN HISTORY PRIZE 2018–2019
selected by
Dr Kristyn Harman, Dr Imogen Wegman,
Dr Nick Brodie and Chris Champion

© 2019
Copyright remains with the individual authors

ISBN 978-0-6485328-5-9

All rights reserved.
Without limiting the rights under copyright above, no part of this publication may be reproduced, stored in or introduced into a retrieval system, or transmitted in any form or by any means (electronic, mechanical, photocopying, recording or otherwise), without the prior written permission of the relevant author.

Published by Forty South Publishing Pty Ltd, Hobart, Tasmania
www.fortysouth.com.au

Printed by IngramSpark

Cover image: George and Matilda Wainwright, centre, at Mount Cameron, c.1900. (Detail)
Courtesy Kath Medwin

Title page image: Following the eclipse, the Port Davey party speedily dismantled their observatory. By this time, the ground had been trampled to a veritable quagmire. (Detail)
From "Eclipse Expedition to Port Davey, 1910" photographic album, Queen Victoria Museum & Art Gallery Community History Collection (QVM:2007:P:0001).

CONTENTS

    Competition judges   vii
    Anthology contributors   viii

Paige Gleeson
    The fantasy of the past   1

Tony Fenton
    Eclipse   10

Terry Mulhern
    St Valentine's tears   19

Claire Doran
    No passengers in the coach   31

Dr Billy Griffiths
    How archaeology helped save the Franklin River   40

Nic Haygarth
    The passing of the "tigerman"   48

Terry Newman
    Constitution Dock: construction, naming and tragedies   57

Amelia O'Donnell
    Growing up at the Triabunna Barracks   66

Gina Slevec
    The enigma of the Midlands arch   81

Kees Wierenga
    Job in Tasmania   92

    Publication history   102

COMPETITION JUDGES

DR KRISTYN HARMAN is an Associate Professor in History at the University of Tasmania. Her research interests cohere around socio-cultural frontiers including: transportation to, and within, British colonies; frontier warfare; Indigenous incarceration; and the Australian and New Zealand home fronts during World War II. She is the author of *Cleansing the Colony: Transporting Convicts from New Zealand to Van Diemen's Land* (2017), longlisted for the Royal Society Te Aparangi Award in the Ockham New Zealand Book Awards, 2018. In 2014, Kristyn won the Australian Historical Association Kay Daniels award for her first book, *Aboriginal Convicts: Australian, Khoisan, and Māori Exiles* (2012).

DR IMOGEN WEGMAN is a historian who explores the stories under our feet through historical maps and landscapes. Her PhD thesis looked at land granting in Van Diemen's Land, examining the differences between emancipist and free settler grants, and how they related to the deeper history of the island. She holds several jobs, some in historical research and some in history communication, and is an organiser of Hobart's monthly Pint of History events at Shambles Brewery. When not poring over maps, Imogen can be found reading narrative nonfiction or exploring the urban streets and bush tracks.

DR NICK BRODIE is a historian, archaeologist and writer. His PhD dissertation was in medieval poor laws, but he has since gone on to write a suite of books of Australian history, including *1787: The Lost Chapters of Australia's Beginnings* and *The Vandemonian War: The Secret History of Britain's Tasmanian Invasion*. He regularly contributes articles about Tasmanian history to *Tasmania 40°South*.

CHRIS CHAMPION is editor of *Tasmania 40°South* and a director of Forty South Publishing with responsibility for all editorial functions. He has worked as an editor in Australia and Asia for more than 40 years. The historians on the judging panel were asked to assess all entries and create a short list based on the merit of their historical investigation and examination. Chris then chose the winner based on the second criterion in The Van Diemen History Prize, writing quality.

ANTHOLOGY CONTRIBUTORS

PAIGE GLEESON is a sixth generation Tasmanian and PhD Candidate in History at the University of Tasmania. Paige researches the history of imperial visual culture and museums, and writes about contemporary art and Australian culture. Paige's research interests include feminism and women's history, Indigenous histories of Australia and the Pacific, art in practice and theory, and memory and memorialisation.

TONY FENTON majored in Physics and Computer Science at the University of Tasmania and completed a Graduate Diploma in Information Management. He has devoted most of his time to historical research and writing and his long-standing interest in South West Tasmania — brought about by his grandfather, the legendary tin-miner and naturalist Deny King — led to an exhaustive study of the history of Port Davey. Tony's first book, *A History of Port Davey, South West Tasmania, Volume 1: Fleeting Hopes* (Forty South Publishing, 2017), was shortlisted in the inaugural Dick and Joan Green Family Award for Tasmanian History in 2018 and longlisted in the 2017 Tasmanian Premier's Literary Prizes, Margaret Scott Prize.

TERRY MULHERN is an educator and researcher at the University of Melbourne. If you can't find Terry in his office or somewhere taking a class, look for him in the basement of the University of Melbourne's Baillieu Library under 994.6 History, Tasmania. Terry was born in north Queensland, has worked at universities in the UK and around Australia, but his heart is in northwest Tasmania. He is a regular contributor to *Tasmania 40°South* magazine.

CLAIRE DORAN came to Tasmania from the UK at the age of five and grew up on the Eastern Shore of Hobart. In her forties she started researching her family tree and recently completed the "creative writing" part of the online Diploma in Family History (University of Tasmania). In Grade 5 at Howrah Primary School her teacher, Mr Geeves, was in his last year of a long teaching career. He was one of the Geeveston Geeves and he could tell stories! He's the one who showed Doran how fascinating history could be, but she never followed it as a career. Now that she is approaching retirement, she thinks there might be a story in her somewhere.

DR BILLY GRIFFITHS is a historian and research fellow at the Alfred Deakin Institute for Citizenship and Globalisation, and an Associate Investigator with the Australian Research Council's Centre of Excellence for Australian Biodiversity and Heritage (CABAH). He is the author of *Deep Time Dreaming: uncovering ancient Australia* (Black Inc., 2018) — Book of the Year, 2019 NSW Premier's Literary Award — and *The China Breakthrough: Whitlam in the Middle Kingdom, 1971* (Monash University Publishing, 2012). He is also co-editor with Mike Smith of *The Australian Archaeologist's Book of Quotations* (Monash University Publishing, 2015).

NIC HAYGARTH is a professional historian and freelance writer who was awarded a PhD in History by the University of Tasmania. A prolific author, his most recent publications include *Mountain Men: stories from the Tasmanian High Country* (with Simon Cubit, 2015), *Wonderstruck: treasuring Tasmania's caves and karst* (2015) and *On the Ossie: Tasmanian osmiridium and the fountain pen industry* (2017) — all published by Forty South Publishing. Nic is particularly passionate about Tasmania's wild places, high country and those who populate such areas.

TERRY NEWMAN served 35 years at the Tasmanian Parliamentary Library, with a stint as researcher for the Beaumont Royal Commission into Tasmania's Constitution. After becoming Parliamentary Librarian he eventually retired as Parliamentary Historian. During these decades Terry amassed a lengthy bibiliography of journal articles, several in the London-based *Parliamentarian*. He wrote a history of daylight saving "About Time" for the Royal Society and corrected the commencement date for Tasmania's secret ballot (1856). For public benefit he compiled fact sheets and entries for Parliament's website and seven reference works. These included *Hare-Clark in Tasmania: representation of all opinions* and *Becoming Tasmania: renaming Van Diemen's Land*. He also contributed several entries in the Companion to Tasmanian History.

AMELIA O'DONNELL is a current Master of Arts research student at The University of Sydney. Her research critiques and seeks to expand the current interpretive conventions employed by Australian historical archaeologists in their material culture-based studies of past children and childhoods. Amelia's interest in the lives of past children was piqued after a handful of unexpected children's artefacts were found during her first "proper" archaeological dig as an undergraduate student with the Australian National University in 2016.

GINA SLEVEC is a teacher of Senior English in Launceston, with a passion for creative writing. In 2013 she completed her MA (Creative Writing) at UTAS under Rohan Wilson. Growing up amidst beautiful old homes in the historic town of Evandale, Tasmania, along with the stories of her own personal ancestry in the Norfolk Plains area, fostered an enduring fascination with Tasmania's colonial history. When free time can be found, she is exploring her love of uncovering these stories of Tasmania's yesteryear, relishing in researching information on the people and places of our past. The draft of her first novel is near completion, and she continues to experiment with short fiction and non-fiction.

KEES WIERENGA was born in Hobart to Dutch migrants. He worked in retail locally, interstate and in the Netherlands and eventually owned a Mitre10 hardware shop, with a partner. He devised the PLU numbering system that allowed timber and cladding sales and stock to be controlled with computerised point of sale systems, which is still used today. In 2005 Kees gained a BA (Hons) with a focus on Dutch migrants to Tasmania. He is curator of the Dutch migrant display in the Channel Museum, Margate and editor of the website DutchTasmanianConnection. He co-authored, with Ian Spence, *The Electrona Carbide Works 100 Years* and is now researching the history of the church in Kingston.

WINNER, 2019 VAN DIEMEN HISTORY PRIZE

The fantasy of the past
Women's history at the Cascades Female Factory
PAIGE GLEESON

"I do not think we can begin to understand women's position in Australia today, nor men's attitudes to women, without at least a cursory consideration of those past events and ideas which cast shadows on the present."
— Anne Summers [1]

The site of the Cascades Female Factory is swamped in the cold shadows of autumn dusk long before the rest of the town. An inky blue mountain and steep hillsides lined with weatherboard houses encase what remains of the site. It is situated at the bottom of a valley, alongside a creek that runs down off Mt Wellington/kunanyi, known to expand in streams of floodwater to envelop the factory site itself during heavy rain. Even in drier times, a wetness lingers in the air once the noon sun passes, leaving a smell of damp sandstone, though few Colonial buildings remain standing.

It was here in the early 1840s a group of 300 convict women was reported to have turned in unison to flash backsides at the most important man in Van Diemen's Land, Governor John Franklin, slapping their buttocks like bongo drums.

Hundreds of convict women mooning the Governor and Lady Franklin is a powerful image, and a brilliant leitmotif of female convict rebellion. Bristling at authority and rejecting the stringent social hierarchies of Britain, Tasmanians in particular have reason to identify with this tale of the criminal underclass, given an estimated 74 per cent of us, myself included, are descended from convict stock, the highest rate in the country.[2] It is arguable that a Tasmanian underclass has in many ways remained, the convict stain transformed into a cultural cringe derived from Tasmania's own brand of provincialism and socio-economic depression, frequently tapped into by mainland visitors in the form of two-headed Tasmanian jokes.

That a mythology has developed around The Flashing is seemingly unsurprising given Australia's anti-authoritarian roots and long love affair with larrikinism, though for a group of women to land the starring role is unusual. In our masculinist national mythology, the larrikins are bushrangers, stockmen and military heroes. Yet the Great Mooning was repeatedly cited by historians for years and was subject to a visual depiction by local artist Peter Gouldthorpe that was widely circulated as a postcard, becoming something of a local legend. Why do we have such a collective obsession with convict lady butt?

Before considering this question, it's important to note that the event never actually occurred. If the Franklins ever did eye a convict woman's backside, it was not as this tale relayed it. The mooning was a myth that had taken on a life of its own. A Colonial era manuscript which contained the story was mistaken for a genuine account by historians associated with the University of Tasmania in the 1950s. This manuscript was in fact a novel.

The proliferation of this tale has been used to criticise the empiricism of feminist historians, who relished its rebellion, charging them with a loose retelling of the facts to bolster partisan feminist politics and continue the infiltration of women's history into universities.[3] Indeed, there has been fresh consideration of the lives and social positions of women over the past 40 years thanks to feminist scholars, and convict women have featured prominently in these emergent discourses in Australia.[4] Convict women had previously only received historical mention in relation to male convicts, Colonial administrations, or in order for their sexualities and characters to be morally condemned.[5] As Tamsin O'Connor has claimed, "The harshest criticism — at least until second wave feminists launched their attack — was invariably reserved for the female convicts."[6] It seems we have a preoccupation with women who break the rules.

But if not rebellious bum flashers, who were the women of the Cascades Female Factory, for so long subject to moral condemnation, or erased from history all together? Why are we so obsessed with their characters, in trying to determine whether they were good or bad, Madonnas or whores, measuring their success "in terms of the establishment of the bourgeois nuclear family", as historian Joy Damousi has suggested?[7] Do modern women look backward searching for glimpses of ourselves, projecting false feminist fantasies and falling through the looking glass? Convict women remain today a type of spectacle, as they were in the 1840s amidst media-fuelled hysteria about their behaviour.

∎

In March 1842, the superintendent of the Cascades Female Factory, Mr Hutchinson, stood hidden in a doorway watching a group of six naked, dancing convict women. Mr Hutchinson reported that he was quite horrified by what he saw, though he observed the nude scene for several minutes before announcing himself. In his testimony to the Committee of Inquiry into Female Convict Discipline 1841–1843, Mr Hutchinson reported the women were "dancing perfectly naked, and making obscene attitudes towards each other; they were also singing and shouting and making use of most disgusting language".[8] Upon Mr Hutchinson revealing himself, the women innocently claimed they were merely bathing. Mr Hutchinson was not fooled by this, arguing that there was not a wash tub in sight.[9] The women, he stated, were making the most repulsive gestures to each other in "imitation of men and women together".[10] Considered a scandalous offence by the authorities of the time, this supposed bathing ritual was one of many incidents that saw the establishment of the Van Diemen's Land government's Inquiry into Female Convict Discipline. The inquiry's investigative committee was charged with reviewing female convict behaviour inside the colony's female factories after significant media scrutiny and public pressure.

A group of convict women from the Cascades factory in the late 1830s and early 1840s, dubbed The Flash Mob by local media, become a thorn in the government's side. While the horrors of convict life are well documented in popular contemporary representations, this group of women was reported to have developed a taste for life on the inside. They dressed in "flash" (fancy) clothing and jewellery (inspiring the name "flash mob"), drank alcohol and smoked tobacco smuggled into the factory, and many had sexual relationships with each other. They were, reported the *Colonial Times*, of the belief that "they could 'bowl off' their three or four months [at the Factory] with the greatest ease; laugh at the Magistrate, and skip out of the office with the utmost nonchalance".[11]

It was the editor of the *Colonial Times,* John Campbell Macdougall, who led the media charge against the government's handling of these women, fanning the easily ignitable flames of moral outrage. In March 1840, Macdougall released a scathing and salacious article titled "The Female Factory — The Flash Mob!" which made allegations of misconduct among female convicts at the Cascades Female Factory. Macdougall claimed he did not wish to sully the minds of readers with the intimate details of what had been occurring at the factory, stating, "few, indeed, of any who possess the ordinary attributes of human nature, can even conjecture the frightful abominations, which are practiced by the women, who compose this mob".[12]

However, he promptly abandoned his own reservations, referring to the female convicts as "annoying and untractable animals", and divulging scandalous details of the horrors alleged to be taking place at the factory under cover of darkness.[13] The horrors referred to were lesbian sexual activity between the women, and the consumption of the "indulgences" of tobacco and alcohol, that were easily procured at the factory thanks to the Flash Mob.[14]

MacDougall, in his sensationalist fervour, goes so far as to compare the daily activities of the Flash Mob to Saturnalia, an ancient Roman festival where social norms are completely, but temporarily, overturned. The article concludes by demanding an investigation into the running of the factory to address the "palpable negligence" of its operation, and boldly asks if the Superintendent, Mr Hutchinson, is "(!) afraid of these harpies?"[15] It is unlikely that Mr Hutchinson was indeed afraid of the women, though he did have a penchant for watching them naked while lingering unseen in doorways. His actions symbolically allude to the male sexual eye frequently cast over the lives and behaviour of convict women, and that has for the longest time played the defining role in their characterisation.[16]

The sexual improprieties occurring at the factory that so obsessed Macdougall in 1840 continued into 1842 and 1843. The Principal Superintendent of Convicts, Josiah Spode, submitted testimony to the inquiry in February 1843 that claimed 12 months previously two women "had been detected in the very act of exciting each other's passions — on the Lord's day in the House of God — and at the very time divine service was performing".[17] In addition to the excitation of the absolute wrong type of passion in church, 1842 to 1843 saw two riots and two vicious sexual assaults committed by women on other women at the factory.[18] What emerges from these accounts is an at times frustratingly complex picture of convict women and their lives. This complexity derives not only from the actions of the women, but from our own expectations of them.

■

For the Colonial authorities of the 1840s, badly behaved women presented a peculiar moral dilemma. While convict women were marked as disorderly and depraved, it was not considered appropriate for women to be physically disciplined in the same manner as men. Convict women frequently rejected the social conventions of femininity assigned to their sex, but male Colonial authorities could not conceive of violating the social conventions of femininity that they held so sacrosanct. It was the women's rejection of these conventions that necessitated their punishment in the first instance and from which the authorities wished to see them reformed. Physical violence was not a favoured option, a contradiction seemingly too vulgar, but how then were the authorities to punish such women and quell the behaviour detailed in the Inquiry? In July 1845, *The Observer* quotes a dispatch to the local government from Edward Smith-Stanley in Britain, who summarises the dilemma and suggests a solution: "The difficulties are greater, inasmuch as those with whom we have to deal are in general as fully depraved as the male convicts, while it is impossible to subject them to the same course of discipline, and thus no alternative seems to be left but either to detain them in actual confinement or to permit them to enter, in some mode or other, into the mass of the population." [19]

Yet the suffering inflicted by solitary confinement carried its own challenges. Many of the riots that occurred at the female factories in Van Diemen's Land were a direct response to this form of punishment. The threat of confinement of a member of the Cascades Female Factory's Flash Mob, Catherine Owens, described in the inquiry as an "extremely bad character",[20] lead to a riot in 1842. Eighty-five women barricaded themselves inside the factory, and the police summoned were "beaten off by the women who had armed themselves with the spindle and leg, from the Spinning Wheels, Bricks taken from the floors and walls of the Building, Knives Forks &c and also Quart Bottles in which some of them had received Medicine".[21]

It is stated within the inquiry that due to the women's "excitement", the superintendent thought the best course of action would be to leave them for a time in the hope that they would calm, but instructed the keeper of the factory to deny the women food and water. Given the severity of the escalation, it is possible that the superintendent had no choice but to leave the women as they were. The barricade remained standing overnight, and riotous behaviour, including furniture breaking and fire setting, continued into the following morning until a large barrage of police could be summoned to put an end the stand-off.[22] Negotiations were not entered into, all the women involved were punished, and Owens was placed in solitary as promised.

While the highly restrictive and prescribed gender roles of this era had a notable impact on the lives of convict women, what is reflected is not a dichotomy of "good" or "bad" women, but a system guided by a male eye, stacked against them from the start.[23] Their attempts to navigate this system and their resistance to rigid gender prescriptions account for the borderline hysterical reaction of Macdougall in the *Colonial Times,* Mr Hutchinson's concealed doorway observations, and Stanley's punishing moral dilemma. Convict women were seen as such horrific aberrations because they flouted a male authority that was deeply invested in the social control of women, particularly those indelibly marked as deviant who acted outside the acceptable confines of bourgeois femininity. They incited in ruling class men a subtle fear, and became a spectacle through which such men could reinforce, enact and perform their positions and power.[24]

■

In light of the inquiry's evidence, the story of three hundred women flashing their backsides at the Colonial authorities seems not so flagrant or misleading a fabrication. It effectively symbolises the attitudes of many female convicts and the smaller rebellions that took place at the Cascades Female Factory and the other two female factories in Van Diemen's Land, which are at least verifiable as far as the 1840s are concerned. The riots and behaviour of women at the Cascades Female Factory were bold expressions of contempt for the authorities. Yet they also show how little impact such rebellions had, the immovability and power of Colonial gender roles. Negotiations with the women were never entered into. Rebellion, agency, oppression and victimhood were not mutually exclusive.

More than 150 years later, we often find ourselves steeped in the muck of the Madonna or whore dichotomy in our attempts to understand convict women; the foundations remain firm even as the furniture is moved.

One of Rowan Gillespie's sculptures at Hobart's Macquarie Wharf in 2017.
Photograph courtesy Footsteps Towards Freedom.

The women of the female factory were for many years the butt of jokes, recast for modern audiences in the form of a postcard as the rebellious and "insolent hussies" they were accused of being in 1840. Now they are frequently cast as our brave foremothers, women to memorialise and be proud of. The mythology of the Great Mooning and our preoccupation with the characters of convict women has remained the only constant. We use them in the present as decorations in our chosen narratives of the past. How convict women have been written about and understood says as much, if not more, about us as it does about them. Our fantasies projected backwards bring them to life, colour them real, and mould them to fit the discussions we wish to have.

The darker recesses of the Australian popular imagination are often found folded into Tasmanian corners. The mass suffering of convicts trapped on an island prison, the extinction of the thylacine, the dispossession of the Tasmanian Aboriginal population, the environmental destruction of hydro dams and deforestation, have all contributed to the rise to the term "Tasmanian gothic" in recent years. The plight of female convicts now provides a source of inspiration for this flourishing cultural phenomenon. It has led to a greater sense of connection between us and them, and more sympathetic depictions of the women. Sculptor Rowan Gillespie's 2017 rendering of Irish convict women on Hobart's waterfront, installed at the very point where the women departed ships more than a century before, is a moving and sensitive tribute.

Our collective relationship with convict women, however, was not always so tender and reflective, as sources from the 1840s show. Responses to female convicts over the course of Van Diemonian-Tasmanian history have been mixed and contentious, but it is the work of feminist historians that has allowed women of the past to be imaginatively re-cast as worthy of inclusion and inquiry. They have located women in the past and re-positioned them within our national narratives, challenging the moralistic interpretations of women's lives and behaviour that continue to impact upon women today.

Are these interpretations fact, fabrication, or fantasy? They are no more fantastical than any other historical re-telling, only this time it is women who have spoken.

■ ■ ■

ENDNOTES

1. Anne Summers, *Damned Whores and God's Police: The Colonization of Women in Australia* (Ringwood: Penguin Books, 1975), 60.
2. Merran Williams, "Stain or Badge of Honour? Convict Heritage Inspires Mixed Feelings", The Conversation, accessed 17 September 2018, https://theconversation.com/stain-or-badge-of-honour-convict-heritage-inspires-mixed-feelings-41097.
3. Michael Connor, "Fabricated Feminist Flashers", *The Quadrant*, (May 2010), 56–59.
4. Summers, *Damned Whores* (1975); Miriam Dixson, *The Real Matilda: Women and Identity in Australia 1788 to the Present* (Ringwood: Penguin Books Australia, 1976); Joy Damousi, *Depraved and Disorderly: Female Convicts, Sexuality and Gender in Colonial Australia* (Cambridge: New York: Cambridge University Press, 1997); Kay Daniels, *Convict Women* (Sydney: Allen & Unwin, 1998); Lyndall Ryan, "Reconceptualising Convict Women," *Australian Feminist Studies* 13, No.1 (1998): 143–144; Lucy Frost, *Abandoned Women: Scottish Convicts Exiled Beyond the Seas* (Crows Nest: Allen and Unwin, 2012); Alison Alexander (ed), *Repression, Reform and Resilience: A History of the Cascades Female Factory* (Hobart: Convict Women's Press, 2016).

5. Summers, *Damned Whores,* 319.
6. Tamsin O'Connor, "Depraved and Disorderly: Female Convicts, Sexuality and Gender in Colonial Australia", review of *Depraved and Disorderly* by Joy Damousi, *Journal of Social History* 32, No. 4, 1999, 954.
7. Joy Damousi, "'Depravity and Disorder': The Sexuality of Convict Women," *Labour History*, No.68 (May 1995), 30–45.
8. Colonial Secretary, Franklin Period, Correspondence Files, *Committee of Inquiry into Female Convict Discipline 1841-1843*, TAHO, CSO 22/1/50, No. 169–208, 275.
9. *Committee Inquiry*, 275.
10. *Committee Inquiry*, 275–276.
11. John Campbell MacDougall, "Female Servants," *Colonial Times*, February 18, 1840, 4; https://trove.nla.gov.au/newspaper/article/8750507, accessed July 12, 2018.
12. John Campbell Macdougall, "Female Factory — The Flash Mob!" *Colonial Times*, March 10, 1840, 4; http://nla.gov.au/nla.news-article8750568, accessed September 10, 2018.
13. Macdougall, "Female Factory", 4.
14. Macdougall, "Female Factory", 4.
15. Macdougall, "Female Factory", 4.
16. Marilyn Lake, "Convict Women as Objects of Male Vision: An Historiographical Review", *Bulletin of The Centre for Tasmanian Historical Studies* 2, No. 1 (1988), 40–48.
17. *Committee Inquiry*, 342–343.
18. *Committee Inquiry*, 405–509 and 423–427.
19. J. F. Halles, "The Case of Female Prisoners in Van Diemen's Land", *The Observer and Van Diemen's Land Journal of Politics, Agriculture, Commercial and General Intelligence*, July 4, 1845, 2–3; https://trove.nla.gov.au/newspaper/article/62134955, accessed July 6, 2018.
20. *Committee Inquiry*, 381.
21. *Committee Inquiry*, 383.
22. *Committee Inquiry*, 385.
23. Lake, *Convict Women as Objects of Male Vision*, 40–48.
24. Joy Damousi, "Depravity and Disorder," *Labour History* (1995), 32; Anne McClinktock, *Imperial Leather: Race, Gender and Sexuality in the Colonial Conquest* (New York: Routledge, 1995); Catherine Hall, "Of Gender and Empire: Reflections on the Nineteenth Century," in *Gender and Empire*, ed Philippa Levine (Oxford: New York: Oxford University Press, 2004), 46–76; Philippa Levine, "Sexuality, Gender and Empire", (ed.) P. Levine, *Gender and Empire* (Oxford: New York: Oxford University Press: 2004), 134–155.

HIGHLY COMMENDED, 2019 VAN DIEMEN HISTORY PRIZE

Eclipse

TONY FENTON

How strange, even frightening, a solar eclipse must have seemed to people before its cause was known. So powerful was the effect that omens good or ill have been ascribed to the phenomenon. It might portend the death of a king, for example. Yet for thousands of years we have been able to predict, albeit inexactly at first, when an eclipse might occur. Since the time of Johannes Kepler in the early 17th century, the celestial mechanics has been well understood. The earth orbits the sun and the moon orbits the earth. When the three fall into a sun-moon-earth line, a solar eclipse occurs. But it doesn't happen at every new moon as one might expect, because the moon's orbit around the earth is tilted relative to the earth's orbit around the sun. The rate is more like every six months. It turns out that every 173 days there is an "eclipse season", a period when one, or occasionally two, solar eclipses will occur somewhere in the world. There are other variables, too: depending on how close the earth is to the sun (it varies by some 50,000 kilometres), and on how precisely the three bodies align, the eclipse may be total or partial, annular or crescent.[1]

While the movement of celestial bodies has been understood for hundreds of years, little was known about the sun itself until the late 19th century. Is it composed of the same stuff as found on earth, or something completely different? Is it the same throughout, or does it have layers of different materials? Joseph von Fraunhofer discovered in 1817 that when light is passed through a prism and split into a rainbow, the spectrum — far from being uniform — is a series of lines. These lines, it was subsequently found, depended on the material emitting the light. Different elements left a different set of "fingerprints" on the spectrum. It was only natural that attention should turn to sunlight.

Many of the lines in sunlight matched those catalogued in the laboratory, but there were others, too. In 1869 astronomer Norman Lockyer and others demonstrated that a line in the yellow part of the solar spectrum was caused by an element then unknown on earth. They named it helium, and by the end of the century it had been isolated on earth. Another proposed element was "coronium", to account for certain lines observed during eclipses in the spectrum of the sun's surrounding corona. There seemed to be nothing in the periodic table which could explain the observations, and the idea of the mysterious "coronium" persisted. It was not until the 1960s that the lines were demonstrated to originate from highly ionised iron, which can only exist at temperatures way above anything possible on earth. So spectroscopy has its pitfalls.[2]

The mysteries of the corona occupied the astronomical community around the turn of the century. At each total eclipse, astronomers would record the structure of the corona, and photograph the spectrum for later analysis.

The eclipse predicted for May 9, 1910, would be visible from Australia, the Southern Ocean and some of Antarctica; however the path of totality would extend only from southern Tasmania to Antarctica. Sending an expedition to Antarctica was out of the question. In Tasmania, the eclipse would be late in the day when the sun was only eight degrees above the horizon. Considering the often inclement weather at that time of year, the Royal Astronomical Society (in London) decided not to mount an official expedition to observe the event. However, the Australasian Association for the Advancement of Science did organise an expedition.

The English society lent its instruments to the Australian party led by Pietro Baracchi, the government astronomer of Victoria. The team was comprised of contingents from Melbourne, Adelaide and sundry individuals from all around Australia, including Professor Alex McAulay from the University of Tasmania. Baracchi selected an observation site at Alonnah, on southern Bruny Island, from where the sun would be seen to set at a low point in the skyline. Being on the shore of D'Entrecasteaux Channel, in those days a waterway busy with local shipping, they would be within easy reach of Hobart.

There they set up their instruments: coelostats (sun telescopes), coronagraphs, and sundry mirrors, telescopes, cameras and clocks. A temporary telegraph line was even erected between the camp and the local post office so that the observers could exchange time signals with the Melbourne Observatory through the telegraph network. This greatly simplified determining the longitude of their site and the all-important timekeeping during the eclipse. The men had some difficulty getting a steady foundation for their instruments due to the springy soil; the solution was to remove the 60 centimetres of topsoil and set some large flat boulders found nearby into the holes.[3]

■

Meanwhile an unofficial party, led by an English amateur astronomer, was at work at Port Davey in the south-western corner of Tasmania. Francis Kennedy McClean was a pioneer aviator, beginning his career in 1907 in a balloon race in Berlin. From 1909 he began co-operating with leading aeroplane manufacturer Short Brothers, which built all but one of the 16 aircraft he owned before 1914. He also allowed the Admiralty to use his airfields for training purposes. One of McClean's notable feats was a flight down the River Thames in 1912 in a float plane, in which he flew under London Bridge and between the upper and lower decks of Tower Bridge.[4]

With a keen interest in astronomy fostered by his father (an astronomer who had pioneered objective prism spectrography) and the adventuring spirit that characterised the early aviators, McClean was well-placed to lead an expedition to the ends of the earth to observe an eclipse. Besides, he had been an assistant on an eclipse expedition to Majorca in 1905. Three years later he led an eclipse expedition to Flint Island in the mid Pacific Ocean.[5]

Learning that the Astronomical Society was not going to send a delegation, he decided to mount an expedition himself. After arriving in Tasmania, McClean, along with some of his co-expeditionists, scouted the south-eastern corner of the island. McClean saw merit in setting up his observatory in a different locality from the Australian team; spreading out increased the chances of *someone* observing the eclipse, even if others were prevented by poor weather.

So McClean and his men travelled by train to Strahan where they embarked on the regular West Coast steamer SS *Wainui* for a reconnaissance trip to Port Davey in the remote south-western corner of the State. There they selected a site on the northern side of Bathurst Channel, on the summit of buttongrass-clad Hixon Point at 30 metres above sea level, from which the skyline was very low at the crucial bearing WNW. The steamer then returned the group to Hobart in order to purchase stores, tents and equipment for an extended stay at Port Davey. They also arranged with the Union Steamship Company for Wainui to call in at Port Davey each time she passed: their only contact with the outside world.[6]

McClean's party embarked once more for Port Davey on April 9, fully one month before the eclipse, with 120 heavy crates, cases, bags and boxes plus private kit. The next day Wainui steamed into Bathurst Channel, Port Davey. Now they faced the challenge of unloading the precious equipment by dinghy, they had to haul the heavy instruments in their awkward wooden crates out of the dinghy and up the steep bank using block and tackle with planks as skids. Meanwhile a campsite had been selected in a sheltered patch of scrub at the head of nearby Aladdin Bay. Here the problems were different: the shallow bay meant that the boat had to land further away and tents and stores had to be lugged for 50 metres along the jagged quartzite foreshore rocks to the campsite.

It took five hours to land the personnel, stores and equipment, after which Wainui steamed away, leaving the party in splendid isolation. But not quite: Two tin miners from Cox Bight on the South Coast happened to be hunting in the area when the expeditionists arrived. These brawny men pitched in, helping to unload and, once the steamer had left, assisted in cutting and benching a track through tangled scrub between the campsite and the observatory.

Lugging the hefty instrument crates up the steep bank to the observatory site took several days. The heavier of these were broken open and the separate castings removed from their protective straw packing to be toted up. On one occasion, a week into their stay, they had left an instrument in its opened crate while they went down to camp for lunch. Three quarters of an hour later billowing smoke was blown from the observatory across the camp. The men rushed up the hill to find a line of fire across the promontory. As they approached the flagpole fell (no expedition is complete without a flagpole), but they managed to save the tent containing most of the instruments. Now the fire raced toward the camp! While a couple of men stayed to protect the equipment, the rest of the team hurried to the camp to rescue their provisions. Luckily the fire stopped at the wet scrub surrounding the camp. Although the greatest danger was now over, the fire had penetrated the peaty soil and continued to smoulder, flaring up from time to time over the next few days. The fire was thought to have started in the straw packing of one of the instruments, though any theories as to source of ignition were not committed to paper. A photograph

One of McClean's men inspects the driving weights of one of the heliostats at the partly set-up observatory. The Union Jack proudly flutters above, lest the local wildlife doubt the party's nationality.

From "Eclipse Expedition to Port Davey, 1910" photographic album, Queen Victoria Museum & Art Gallery Community History Collection (QVM:2007:P:0001).

album in the Queen Victoria Museum and Art Gallery, Launceston, shows the men's habit of smoking pipes while working — perhaps an ember from one dropped into the straw.[7]

Rain, wind and sleet dogged most of their stay, and the ground around the camp and observatory was soon trampled to an "appalling quagmire". Tarpaulins and infrastructure blew down in the gales; even one of the heavy instruments toppled. Against these odds, the party managed to pour concrete bases for the instruments, erect a brushwood windbreak and, during lulls, set up the instruments. A few days prior to the eclipse the weather cleared allowing adjustments to be made.[8]

Unlike the Australian expedition, McClean's party did not have the luxury of a telegraph connection to receive time signals to determine their exact longitude. Instead they had to rely on chronometers, and even the best chronometers of the day did not keep perfect time, making calculations difficult. Nevertheless, by comparing their clock before departing

Following the eclipse, the Port Davey party speedily dismantled their observatory. By this time, the ground had been trampled to a veritable quagmire.

From "Eclipse Expedition to Port Davey, 1910" photographic album, Queen Victoria Museum & Art Gallery Community History Collection (QVM:2007:P:0001).

civilisation and on return, they were able to get a reasonable estimate of their observatory's position. The clear night on May 6 enabled the necessary astronomical observations.[9]

■

The two expeditions had spent months in meticulous preparation for an event which would last a few minutes. In the days prior to the eclipse, both teams repeatedly rehearsed the actions they would need to perform: calling the different phases of the eclipse, counting the seconds, opening and closing shutters, changing photographic plates, and so on. There would only be one chance, and each party had to work as a well-oiled machine.

Late on May 9, 1910, local time, the appointed hour arrived. At Bruny Island, a sunny morning had given way to an overcast afternoon, while at Port Davey the fine weather that had raised the men's hopes a few days earlier reverted once more to steady drizzle, increasing to pelting rain. The situation seemed hopeless.

The camp of the Australasian Association for the Advancement of Science expedition on Bruny Island.
Museum of Applied Arts & Sciences

It was. On account of the unfavourable conditions, the carefully orchestrated program at Port Davey was hastily revised to conserve expensive photographic plates and to maximise the possibility of recording *something*. The men stood stoically by their instruments in the rain. Inexorably the celestial bodies moved into alignment and the sky began to darken. At Bruny Island, GF Dodwell, Government Astronomer of South Australia, noted:

> The scene was fascinating, unique, even weird. The array of military tents and shelter sheds for the instruments; the astronomers within the enclosure, every man at his post ready to perform his allotted tasks; the electric relay with its megaphone attachment beating seconds from a clock so loudly that the seconds could be heard throughout the camp, the timekeeper (Dr Kenny) calling the time during the calculated period; the silent but intensely interested group of spectators outside the enclosure ...[10]

Birds fell silent, dogs howled. The seconds were called, and the beginning of totality announced. Exposures were taken in the vain hope for a small break in the clouds. None came. No doubt disappointed, the expeditionists at both camps began dismantling their equipment almost immediately. Perversely, the weather cleared before sunset, and McClean's men continued packing well into a beautifully starry night. The time, money and effort expended by the two expeditions was in vain, but such is the nature of astronomy.

Although the astronomers could not view what they had come so far to witness, many ordinary people stopped what they where doing for a few moments to watch the phenomenon. There had been a growing public interest in the weeks prior to the event. Even advertisers got in on the act: "A total eclipse. Jones's I.X.L. Jams eclipse all others".[11] In some parts of southern Tasmania the skies were clear, while on mainland Australia, even the partial eclipse was a spectacle deemed worthy of watching.

Queenstown had been discounted by the astronomers as being too close to the northern limit of totality, and its rainfall record was discouraging. The schoolmaster, AG Waterworth, had woven the eclipse into his lessons, and an excursion to Howard Plains was in order. But with the gloomy weather on Monday, May 9, the excursion was cancelled and his pupils were downcast at the thought of not seeing the event they had been so anticipating.

For most of the day the weather at Queenstown was overcast with leaden skies, but at about 3pm a patch of blue appeared in the west, and gradually grew. Townsfolk, who had been resigned to not seeing the eclipse, hastily grabbed cameras or pieces of smoked glass to look through. Waterworth and the children climbed nearby Spion Kop Lookout where the schoolmaster was bombarded with excited questions throughout the two-and-a-half minute totality. A few people managed to take photographs of the eclipse, and these were the only pictures obtained of the event.[12]

But the passengers and crew of RMS *Corinthic* perhaps had the best view. The 12,000-tonne liner was about 1,200 kilometres west-south-west of Hobart en route from London. This put the ship close to the central line of totality, and, being further west, the sun was higher in the sky. The spectacle began at 1:40pm ship's time, with totality commencing about an hour later and lasting four minutes: close to the maximum for that eclipse. The passengers said they saw no coronal "streamers" radiating out from the sun, contradicting eyewitnesses in Queenstown who were adamant they saw them, which gave the astronomers cause to scratch their heads. A few people took snapshots, but these did not come out well.[13]

■

King Edward VII had died just before midnight on May 6; the news did not reach many parts of Tasmania until the day of the eclipse, making the event especially charged for his loyal subjects who witnessed it. At Queenstown, church bells tolled. Those who had heard a few days previously were still affected by the news: "All nature, here at least," wrote Dodwell, "seemed hushed and sympathetic in the passing of a great nation's ruler." But if an eclipse portends a great event, the heavens were a bit behind the times.

▪ ▪ ▪

ENDNOTES

1. Mark Littmann, Fred Espenak and Ken Willcox, *Totality: Eclipses of the Sun* (Oxford: Oxford University Press, 3rd edn, 2008), 10–13.
2. Thomas Crump, *Solar Eclipse: The Path of Darkness — Apocalypse or Portent?* (London: Constable, 1999), 117–128.
3. G. F. Dodwell, *Report to the Hon Minister of Education on the Total Solar Eclipse of the Sun of May 9th, 1910, in Tasmania* (Adelaide: R. E. Rogers, 1910), 3–4.
4. "Francis McClean", Wikipedia, accessed 9 August 2018. https://en.wikipedia.org/wiki/Francis_McClean.
5. Ibid.
6. F. K. McClean et al., *Report of the Solar Eclipse Expedition to Port Davey, Tasmania, May 1910* (London: Richard Clay & Sons, 1910), 2–4.
7. Photographic album of the Eclipse Expedition, 1910, Queen Victoria Museum and Art Gallery Community History Collection (QVM:2007.P.0001).
8. F. K. McClean et al., 11–14.
9. Ibid., 30–37.
10. G. F. Dodwell, 7.
11. *Mercury*, April 9, 1910, 5.
12. *Zeehan & Dundas Herald*, May 11, 1910, 4.
13. G. F. Dodwell, 8; *Daily Post*, May 12, 1910, 7.

HIGHLY COMMENDED, 2019 VAN DIEMEN HISTORY PRIZE

St Valentine's tears

TERRY MULHERN

It's the early hours of Sunday, September 2, 1832 in Circular Head, north-west Van Diemen's Land. Henry Hellyer, chief surveyor and architect with the Van Diemen's Land Company, sits alone in his room. He arrived six years ago, excited by the prospect of finding adventure and making his fortune. Now, he's in a pit of despair — and he's been there for a long time. His self-esteem has been slowly eaten away and he feels an enormous weight of guilt. On Wednesday, he had pleaded for help to deal with his tormentors. But his concerns were dismissed as trivial. On Thursday and Friday, he had put out subtle signals that he was thinking dark and deadly thoughts. But no-one noticed. Now, he locks the door to his room, sits down on his bed and stares at the three things on his desk: an open book, an unfinished map, and the letter he's been writing, changing and rewriting for days.

■

The letter on Hellyer's desk was a jumble of his own words and quotes from the *King James Bible*, *The Book of Common Prayer* and literary sources, including Daniel Defoe's *Robinson Crusoe*. The themes were of a shipwrecked man; struggling in the thrall of evil men; and being hounded to death in a trial without evidence. In her 2010 book *Utmost Extrication*, clinical psychologist Gwyneth Daniel described the psychological autopsy she performed on Hellyer.[1] Daniel analysed Hellyer's diaries, reports and letters, including this one, to characterise his changing word usage from 1826 to 1832.[2] When Hellyer arrived in Van Diemen's Land he wrote eloquently of the beauty of his new home and his diary entries were decorated with sketches of the landscape

(Copy)

In asking myself this question, what evil hath he done? it has occurred to me that labouring under an affliction from a wound that rec'd. the ~~must have been in dressing, it has been~~ of having no one my dressing it, has been misunderstood by any one who may have seen me so employed, ~~and has~~ ~~and that has originated~~ ~~the vile scandal which has~~

But God is the searcher of hearts and in him I put my trust

Let traducers of character beware how they trifle with the feelings of a fellow creature

Hold not thy tongue O God of my praise, for the mouth of the ungodly yea the mouth of the deceitful is opened upon me

And they have spoken against me with false tongues they compassed me about with words of hatred and fought against me without a cause

For the love that I had unto them, lo, they now take a contrary part but I give myself unto prayer

They have they rewarded me evil for good and hatred for my goodwill.

~~But~~ O deliver me for I am helpless and poor and my heart is wounded within me

Forgive my enemies persecutors & slanderers and turn their hearts

No friend to advise with to advise with any thoughts distract me ~~wrote knowing~~ without ~~my~~

If despair ~~not to has one~~ ~~woo help me~~ ~~donot relative Brothers been~~ distracted with the thought of such ~~in a sudden~~ false ~~accus to~~ ~~one which~~

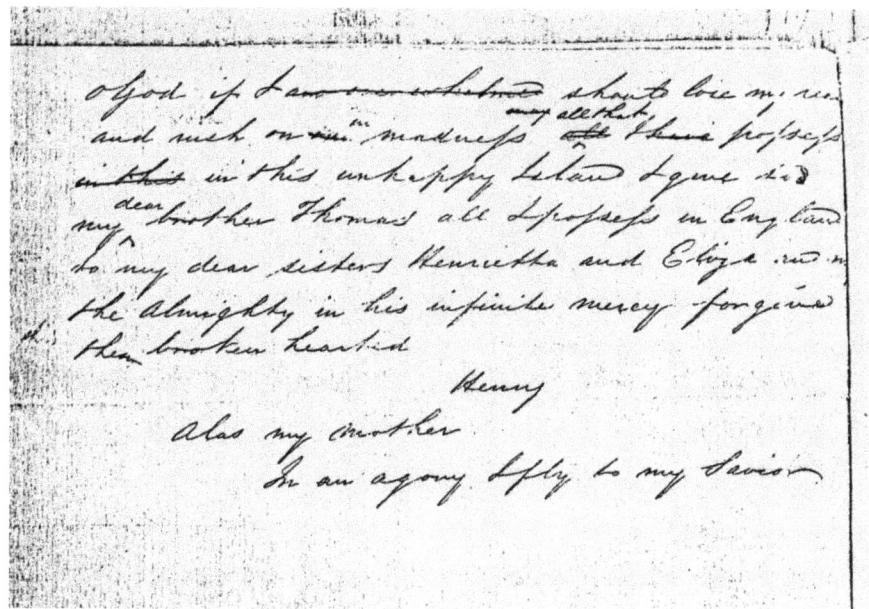

Opposite and above: Copy of Henry Hellyer's suicide note from the inquest notes. The original letter is not in existence, but these are images of a copy made by Edward Curr at the inquest into Hellyer's death in 1832.

NS433/1/1 b. original correspondence — suicide note / VDL Co. surveyor/architect Henry Hellyer's suicide note 1832

and the plants and animals he observed.[3] This changed as the years passed. The illustrations vanished and his writing became gloomy and introspective. Daniel believes Hellyer was suffering from severe depression with anxiety. His illness may have started before he left England, but undoubtedly it worsened steadily during his time in Van Diemen's Land. It also may have been compounded by the neurological impact of the autoimmune disease lupus, as well as post-traumatic stress, brought on by several near-death experiences.

It's clear that Hellyer's depression intensified in the week leading up to this moment of crisis. One or more of the other VDL Co. officers at their headquarters at Circular Head were spreading rumours about him, and he felt unsupported by the company's local manager, Edward Curr. On that Wednesday, Hellyer complained in writing to Curr that "prejudicial reports respecting me" were circulating in the mess. Hellyer suspected that the rumours originated from two convicts, Harley and Ward, members of Hellyer's team that built the bridge over the Wey River. They had sworn revenge against Hellyer for denying them a twenty-shilling bonus after they stole alcohol. While Hellyer was certain that the convicts' motivation was vindictiveness, he wanted to know what the actual rumours were and which "gentleman" was now spreading them. Curr blithely dismissed his request for an investigation, telling Hellyer it was beneath him to be concerned about the words of mere "prisoners". Later, it emerged that the rumour was of a sexual nature. Harley and Ward claimed to have seen Hellyer masturbating, an allegation Hellyer alluded to in his correspondence with Curr and the letter on his desk. Hellyer believed it arose from him being observed tending an infected wound in his groin, an injury confirmed by the company physician, Dr John Hutchinson. Daniel and others have interpreted these events as Hellyer being accused of homosexuality.[4] Such an allegation, whether true or not, would have been devastating in colonial society.

Homosexuality was considered an abomination that festered below the surface of the convict system. "Unmentionable" acts took place between the decks of the prison hulks, in the barracks at night or on the chain gangs out in the bush. Hellyer was just days away from leaving Circular Head to take up a prized government post in the Surveyor General's Office in Hobart. Daniel suggested that the company's bookkeeper, Samuel Anderson, was jealous of Hellyer's appointment and this led him to reignite Harley and Ward's rumours. Instead of a fresh start, Hellyer probably envisaged being ostracised in Hobart and whispered about behind his back. This could have been enough to tip him over the edge, but Hellyer had other phantoms stalking him.

■

In 1988, surveyor Brian Rollins found a copy of the map from Hellyer's desk in the archives of the Tasmanian Department of Main Roads.[5] The map was of the Surrey Hills and Hampshire Hills districts, inland from present-day Burnie. Before his departure from Circular Head, Hellyer needed to complete his official survey of the lands granted by royal charter to the VDL Co. Finishing this map would have been an excruciatingly painful task for Hellyer. It is likely that Hellyer blamed himself, and felt blamed by others, for the company's financial failure trying to rear sheep in the uplands under the shadow of the Black Bluff Range, near Cradle Mountain.

The VDL Co. was one of a number colonial pastoral companies established in order to try and cash in on the English textile boom of the early 19th century. The industrial revolution was gathering pace and the mills of northern England had an insatiable hunger for wool. In 1820, an ambitious young man from Sheffield, Edward Curr, arrived in Hobart Town and began to make a name for himself as a merchant and budding politician. Upon his return to England in 1823, he published a report on the good prospects for agriculture in the new colony.[6] In 1824, the directors of the VDL Co. engaged Curr as their agent and applied to the British government for land in Van Diemen's Land, speculating that they would receive extensive sheep pasture. On the advice of the returning Lieutenant-Governor, William Sorrell, the company was given permission to seek out a quarter of a million acres of land suitable for "pasturage and tillage" in the remote and unexplored northwest.[7] No one knew for sure whether there was much "useful" land in this part of the island. It was a huge gamble. Hellyer and Curr arrived in Hobart from England on March 14, 1826. They spent six weeks procuring convict labourers, provisions, horses and wagons. Then Hellyer and his survey team set out into the unknown.

With the exception of some good pasture at Woolnorth (Cape Grim) and small areas around Circular Head (Stanley) and Emu Bay (Burnie) the northwest was — and still is, for that matter — mostly dense forest, steep mountains and subalpine heath. Over the next two years, Hellyer plunged repeatedly into this wilderness seeking open pasture. He built a reputation as a determined, resourceful and physically tough explorer. His most famous expedition was in early 1827. He set out on foot from Circular Head for the landmark "peak like a volcano" sighted from out at sea by George Bass and Matthew Flinders in 1798.[8] Hellyer and his men forded wild rivers and pushed their way through tangled horizontal scrub. They struggled for days through dark forests where "the foliage is impervious to the rays of the sun".[9] On February 14, Hellyer climbed the mountain and named it St Valentine's Peak. From the summit he saw the open country his employers were so desperate to find. Hellyer named these areas the Surrey and Hampshire Hills in honour of his home in southern England. In his report he described them in glowing terms.

> I found it consisted of grassy hills and knolls, and resembling a neglected old park; a thousand to fifteen hundred acres in a patch, without a tree ... The kangaroos stood gazing at us like fawns, and in some instances came bounding towards us; and if we shouted they ran like a flock of sheep.[10]

Hellyer had climbed "nar.tone.no" and looked out upon "wool.lun.nen.gar".[11] He did not encounter the owners, the Noeteeler, but he knew they were nearby as he entered their huts and poked at the ashes of their campfires.¹² The Noeteeler spent the winter on the Bass Strait coast, between Emu Bay and Port Sorrell, harvesting crayfish, shellfish and waterbirds and their eggs. When the snows melted, they moved inland into the open country around the peak where they would hunt kangaroo, emu and wallaby. For hundreds of generations they kept their lands open and the pasture seasonally refreshed by "firestick farming". They would climb nar.tone.no to mine the blood-red ochre from the craggy peak and use it for adornment, ceremony and to trade with their neighbours.¹³

In a rash and fateful decision, Curr immediately ordered Hellyer to cut a road inland from Emu Bay to the Surrey Hills. In the years to come, Curr would rue not sending the VDL Co.'s Agricultural Superintendent, Alexander Goldie, to confirm Hellyer's exuberant assessment. Hellyer and his men spent a miserable winter in the cold dark forest. They inched their way southward, felling the towering trees and then rolling aside the massive trunks. It rained incessantly and they were forever short of rations. The men's morale declined, Hellyer fell ill and his diary suggests he sank into depression. Eventually, the road was completed and in January 1828. When Curr came to inspect his new possessions, he wasn't impressed with Hellyer's Surrey and Hampshire Hills. The coarse native grasses and damp ground may have been fine for kangaroo and emu, but not for sheep. Curr would later write of Hellyer that if he had one failing, it was that "all his geese were swans".¹⁴ Curr sent Hellyer further inland to search for better pasture. All Hellyer found was more forest and snow-capped mountains. These days, the Surrey and Hampshire Hills are largely under forestry plantations. The land has never been suitable for cropping or livestock — the soils are poor and it's too wet and cold. The winters of 1828–1832 saw the loss of thousands of the VDL Co.'s precious merino sheep.¹⁵ Their bones littered the landscape, but these weren't the only bones that lay hidden among the undergrowth.

■

The last item on Hellyer's desk was a book that Curr gave him to read on Saturday. It was a report from the British House of Commons, detailing the correspondence between Lieutenant-Governor George Arthur and the British Government from 1828–1831 during the "Black War" between the settlers and Aborigines.¹⁶ The war reached its climax in the spring of 1830 when Arthur mobilised his military and the civilian population into what he called "the line". During October, a near continuous cordon of some two thousand armed white men moved across the settled districts from north to south, attempting to drive the remnants of the Big River and Oyster Bay tribes into the natural prison of the Tasman Peninsula. The success or failure of Arthur's grand military operation has been long argued. He himself stated in a dispatch to the Secretary of State for the Colonies, that:

> I regret to report that the measures that I had the honour to lay before you, terminated without the capture of either of the native tribes.[17]

The press ridiculed Arthur's military campaign as an expensive failure.[18] But nonetheless, armed conflict in the eastern settled districts all but ceased. However, the same could not be said on the northwest frontier. There, the guerrilla war between the Aborigines and the VDL Co. continued for more than a year with ambushes and revenge attacks from both sides.[19] While fierce Aboriginal resistance had forced Arthur into unprecedented military action in 1830, more than a year before, Arthur had attempted something else quite extraordinary. In early 1829, he appointed a fellow evangelical Christian, George Augustus Robinson, to "conciliate" with the Aborigines. For five years Robinson traversed the island making contact with the rapidly declining Aboriginal population; convincing them or, if that failed, deceiving them into being transported into exile on the Bass Strait islands.[20] In mid-1830, Hellyer guided Robinson and his band of Aboriginal translators-cum-negotiators, which included Truganini, Woorraddy and Tunnerminnerwait, on a fruitless mid-winter circuit of the Surrey Hills searching for the remnants of the Noeteeler and the other northern clans. Hellyer and Robinson took advantage of a rare clear day to climb St Valentine's Peak. They looked out across the landscape — now largely empty of its traditional owners, barely three years after its "discovery" by Hellyer. Robinson took in the view and reflected on the Aboriginal perspective.

> ... this country must have been a great loss to them, as it abounds with kangaroo.[21]

A key member of Robinson's party was Alexander McKay, a Scottish convict who worked with Hellyer building the road from Emu Bay in 1827. McKay was a renowned bushman and when he left the service of the VDL Co. he was assigned to Robinson's "Friendly Mission". After Hellyer bade farewell to Robinson, McKay told Robinson that Hellyer "would haunt the Surrey Hills after he was dead".[22] Robinson interpreted this as referring to Hellyer's seemly misguided attachment to this "dreary country".[23] But perhaps McKay was hinting at something else — Hellyer's growing guilt about the inevitable failure of the VDL Co.'s sheep farming there. Out of earshot of Hellyer, VDL Co. shepherds had confided to McKay that they were losing up to fifty sheep a month.[23] However, there was also a dreadful human cost. In less than a decade, the war between black and white caused the Aboriginal population on the lands occupied by the VDL Co. to collapse from an estimated seven hundred to a little over one hundred. In stark contrast, only three VDL Co. employees were killed by Aborigines.[24]

By the early 1830s, British Christian humanitarianism was close to realising its goal of abolishing slavery; and its gaze was shifting to the treatment of the Empire's "native" peoples. Many humanitarians believed the natives should be protected from settler violence and "civilized" into British ways.[25] Like Robinson, Hellyer was a devout Christian and was one of the few VDL Co. Officers sympathetic to Robinson's mission to "save" the Aborigines.[26] In mid-1832, Robinson's mission once again took him to the northwest. Robinson and Hellyer met several times and corresponded regularly. A letter from Robinson arrived during that turbulent week. In it, Robinson thanked Hellyer for his "lively interest" in his work, but we have no idea what impact the letter had on Hellyer's state of mind.[27] However, something else that Hellyer's received late that week was to go on to attain unusual prominence — Arthur's book about the Black War.

Curr mentioned the book multiple times in a letter he later wrote to Hellyer's brother Thomas in Hobart. In that letter, Curr described receiving the book from Launceston on Friday afternoon; his passing it on to Hellyer on Saturday morning; that Hellyer discussed the book with a friend late on Saturday evening; and that Hellyer was seen still reading the book after midnight, when a servant came to take his boots away to be cleaned.[28] When Robinson eventually returned to Circular Head many weeks later, Curr let him read the book too.[29]

Arthur's book was reprinted in 1971 by the historian Alan Shaw. Upon reading it, I found Curr's obsession with it all the more intriguing. I expected to find some damning statement about the murderous violence perpetrated by employees of the VDL Co. against Aborigines — and I believe that is what Curr, Hellyer and Robinson expected too. To our collective surprise, it doesn't mention the 1828 Cape Grim massacre where, in retaliation for killing sheep, thirty Aboriginal men and women were shot and their bodies thrown over a cliff into the sea.[30] It does not mention the gruesome axe-murder of an Aboriginal woman at Emu Bay in August 1829.[31] It does not mention the

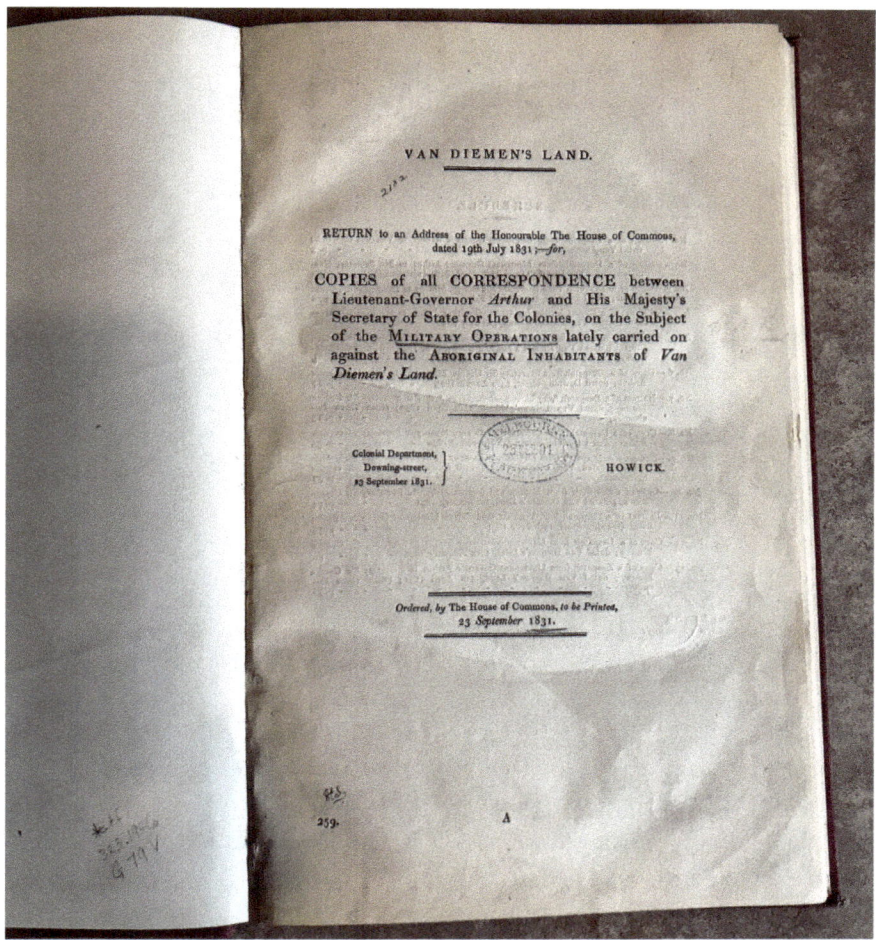

The cover page of the report from the British House of Commons. This is an original 1831 copy of the book held by the State Library of Victoria. I was hoping it was the actual book from Hellyer's desk — but the library kept no provenance for the book and there are no blood spots on it nor indication that it belonged to Edward Curr or his son Edward M Curr (who both moved to Port Phillip District).

LTF 323.1946 G76V, Rare Book Collection, State Library of Victoria

alleged killing of Aborigines during 1830 in the Hampshire and Surrey Hills by "baiting" them with poisoned flour.[32] It does not mention the unprovoked stabbing and disembowelment of an Aboriginal man in September 1830 by a VDL Co. stockkeeper who lured him close by offering him damper.[33] It does not mention Curr's infamous request for his shepherds to bring him the heads of Aborigines to mount atop a hut to warn off others.[34] Undoubtedly, Curr was

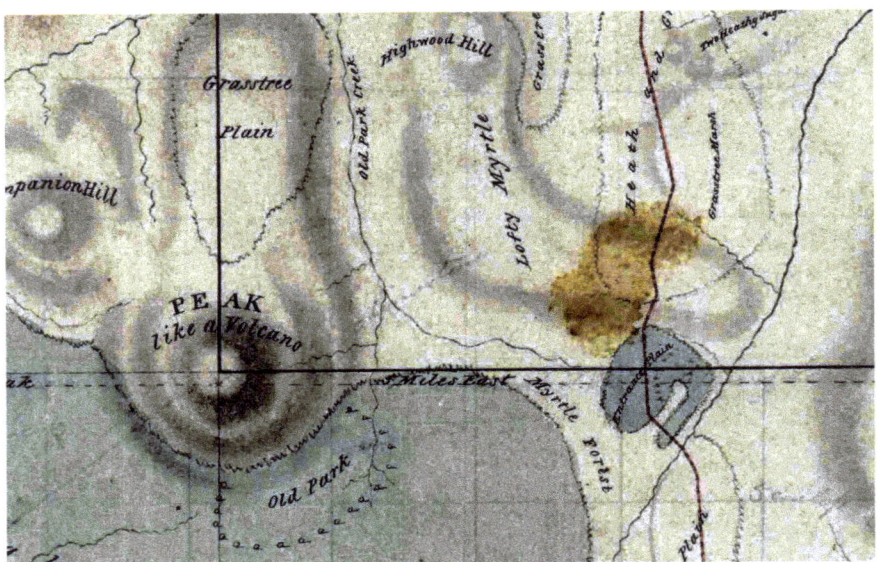

The central section of Henry Hellyer's "Map of the Van Diemen's Land Company's Proposed Eastern Locations, Van Diemen's Land" with the two blood spots next to the "PEAK like a Volcano".
Tasmanian Archives AF396/1/1186[38]

relieved to find that the book neither mentioned him, the VDL Co., nor a single Aboriginal death in the northwest. Back in London, the Directors of the VDL Co. must have been relieved too. Arthur's dispatches were reprinted almost verbatim in their 1832 annual report.[35] We are left to ponder what Hellyer thought, as he pored over this "whitewash", late into the night and then into the early morning.

I believe that the book had a significant impact on the already fragile Hellyer. He does not mention the book in his letter. Perhaps its omissions were too "black" to be discussed openly. Hellyer may not have killed any Aborigines by his own hands, but when he climbed that peak on St Valentine's Day 1827, he was the one who set in motion the train of events which dispossessed the northern Aboriginal people of their ancestral lands. Did his Christian humanitarianism needle him to feel some personal responsibility for all the bloodshed that followed? Robinson suspected something. He wrote in his journal:

> It is singular that Mr Hellyer was reading this book near to his destroying himself.[36]

Henry picks up the pistol and once again feels its lethal weightiness. How many times in the last few days has he put it to his forehead, only to pull it away? Then it all comes flooding over him — accusation, innuendo, whispers, laughter, failure, shame and so much death and misery. He thinks of his mother and tears roll down his cheeks. This time, he does not pull the pistol away. His hand begins to shake, but he squeezes the trigger. The flash and explosion are followed by silence. Two drops of blood fall on the map, just to the east of the "PEAK like a Volcano".[37] The ochre-stained tears of nar.tone.no.

■ ■ ■

ENDNOTES

1. Gwyneth Daniel, *Utmost Extrication: Why Henry Hellyer Shot Himself* (Wynyard, Tas.: Willows Books Publishing, 2010).
2. Jenna L. Baddeley, Gwyneth R. Daniel, and James W. Pennebaker. "How Henry Hellyer's Use of Language Foretold His Suicide." *Crisis* 32 no. 5 (2011), 288–292.
3. Bertram M. Thomas, *Henry Hellyer's Observations: Journals of Life in the Tasmanian Bush 1826–1827* (Latrobe, Tas.: North Down Press, 2011).
4. Joe Lake, *Tasmania's Henry Hellyer: A Drama in Two Acts* (Burnie, Tas.: Hamlet Publishing, 1998); Daniel, *Utmost Extrication*; Thomas, *Henry Hellyer's Observations*.
5. Brian J. Rollins, "Henry Hellyer, Esquire, 1790–1832 Van Diemen's Land Company surveyor in His Footsteps" *Australian Surveyor* 34 no. 2 (1988), 110–114.
6. Edward Curr, *An Account of the Colony of Van Diemen's Land ... for the Use of Emigrants* (London: George Cowie, 1824).
7. James Bischoff, *Sketch of the history of Van Diemen's Land, Illustrated by a Map of the Island and an Account of the Van Diemen's Land Company* (London: John Richardson, Royal Exchange, 1832).
8. Matthew Flinders, *Narrative of the expedition of the Colonial Sloop Norfolk, from Port Jackson through the strait which seperates Van Diemen's Land from New Holland; and from thence round the South Cape back to Port Jackson, Completing the circumnavigation of the former island, With some remarks on the coasts and Harbours / by Matt.w Flinders 2nd Lt. H.M.S. Reliance.* (Historical Records of New South Wales, 1799).
9. Bischoff, *Sketch of the history of Van Diemen's Land*, 166.
10. Ibid., 168.
11. Norman J. B. Plomley, *Tasmanian Aboriginal Place Names,* with the assistance of Caroline Goodall (Launceston, Tas.: Queen Victoria Museum and Art Gallery, 1990).
12. Bischoff, *Sketch of the History of Van Diemen's Land*, 177.

13. Lyndall Ryan, *Tasmanian Aborigines: A History since 1803* (Crows Nest, N.S.W.: Allen & Unwin, 2012), 22–25.
14. Thomas, *Henry Hellyer's Observations*, 162.
15. Ibid., 155.
16. Sir George Arthur, *Van Diemen's Land: copies of all correspondence between Lieutenant-Governor Arthur and His Majesty's Secretary of State for the Colonies, on the subject of the military operations lately carried on against the Aboriginal inhabitants of Van Diemen's Land* (Hobart, Tas.: Tasmanian Historical Research Association, 1971).
17. Ibid., 47.
18. Henry Melville, *The Colonial Times*, Friday 26 November 1830, 2.
19. Plomley, *The Aboriginal / settler clash in Van Diemen's Land, 1803–1831*, N. J. B. Plomley; with the assistance of Martina Smythe and Caroline Goodall (Launceston, Tas.: Queen Victoria Museum and Art Gallery, 1992).
20. George A. Robinson, and Norman J. B. Plomley. *Friendly Mission: the Tasmanian journals and papers of George Augustus Robinson, 1829–1834*, edited by N. J. B. Plomely (Hobart Tas.: Quintus Publishing, 2008).
21. Ibid., 232.
22. Ibid., 233.
23. Ibid.
24. Ian McFarlane, "Aboriginal society in North West Tasmania: Dispossession and Genocide" (PhD thesis. University of Tasmania, 2002), 139.
25. Ryan, *Tasmanian Aborigines*, 153.
26. Robinson and Plomely, *Friendly Mission*, 57, 230–231, 675, 678, 731.
27. Ibid., 678, 731.
28. Thomas, *Henry Hellyer's Observations*, 210.
29. Robinson and Plomely, *Friendly Mission*, 711.
30. Ibid., 216.
31. Ibid., 225.
32. Ibid., 229.
33. Plomley, *The Aboriginal / Settler Clash*, 28.
34. McFarlane, *Aboriginal Society in North West Tasmania*, 125.
35. Bischoff, *Sketch of the History of Van Diemen's Land*, 185–260.
36. Robinson and Plomely, *Friendly Mission*, 711.
37. Henry Hellyer, *Map — Wellington 21 — map of the Van Diemen's Land proposed eastern locations including Emu Bay, Hampshire Hills, Surrey Hills and Middlesex Plains — surveyor Henry Hellyer* (Item number AF396/1/1186. Libraries Tasmania's online collection, 1832).
38. Ibid.

No passengers in the coach

CLAIRE DORAN

New Year's Eve 2016. The usual barbecue and drinks to see out the year at the Buckland property Woodsden, which has been in the Mace family since 1828. I stood chatting with Kathy Mace, watching an impromptu campfire burn a hole in the lawn. The children buzzed around us with sparklers and fluorescent wristbands, human fireflies overcharged with the excitement of staying up late.

Kathy said she would like to show me some diaries written by Frederick Mace, great grandfather of her husband Ross. She disappeared inside and returned with a couple of battered books. *Letts's No. 33 Australasian Rough Diary with a week in an opening, for 1915* was boldly lettered on the beige covering of the first I opened. I did not realise it then, but my first view of that diary started me on a journey back in time.

Fred Mace was born in Sydney in 1847 to Henry, an immigrant from Kent, and Caroline (née Cruttenden). By the time Fred was nine, both his parents were dead, and he was sent to live with his uncle, Thomas Cruttenden, the first "squire of Woodsden". Over the years Thomas had acquired, and been granted, extensive landholdings between Buckland (then known as Prosser's Plains) and the east coast.

Thomas attended to Fred's upbringing and schooling, but otherwise not a great deal is known of Fred's early years. Uncle Thomas eventually installed young Fred in Brockley, the property adjacent to Woodsden, to learn the farming business. The first mention of Fred in connection with this property was in 1870, when Fred was in his early 20s. In October of that year, he advertised in the *Mercury* newspaper[1] for a shepherd. Two years later, Fred was elected to the Spring Bay Council, the start of a long career in public office.

On November 11, 1875, Fred married Emma Lyttleton Davies, daughter of Maria Lyttleton and Reverend Rowland Robert Davies, the retired Archdeacon of Hobart. Fred and Emma set up house at Brockley. For Christmas 1875, his mother-in-law Maria (often referred to as "the Mother") gifted to Fred a *Letts's No. 35 Scribbling Journal* for the following year. The diary-keeping habit began; Fred wrote diaries for every year from 1876 to 1931, the year he died.

As I peered at the pages of 1915 by the light of the campfire, in the garden enclosed by the old stone walls of Thomas Cruttenden's house and farm buildings, I was drawn into Fred's world and hooked by the prospect of the history the diaries would contain. I took the 1914 to 1918 books home with me, promising the family I would transcribe those, at the very least, as we were in the centenary years of World War I. If nothing else, I wanted Ross and Kathy's children to be able to read them, and my first look at the handwriting led me to believe that would require a transcription.

I had thought to transcribe them pretty much as they were written, but I soon realised I would have to use some judicious editing to make them readable.

It took me quite a while to tune my eye to Fred's erratic handwriting. He seemed to like to experiment with different styles, was fond of Random Capital Letters, usually NOT at the start of sentences, and incredibly sparing with his punctuation. This often left me with the dilemma of trying to figure out just what he was saying. The location of a comma can make a world of difference to intent, and sometimes I just had to make my best guess.

> Doing odd jobs cold and wet one passenger in the Coach I think Fred
> Robinson Ernest went up with two people and returned I suppose
> Hill must have met him.

I set to work, and several months later, I had completed 1914-1918 and knew there was now no stopping. I had to go back to 1876 and transcribe them all, otherwise it would be like only reading the middle of a book. Kathy delivered the rest of the diaries and off I went on a daily trip back in time.

■

Frederick Mace, 1896.

WEDNESDAY 5 FEBRUARY 1896

Warm day, at times hot. Wind from the sea. Glass lost a little. In the afternoon, there were two slight showers.

Rather tired today and was not up early. Went up for some mangolds to Tom Fox's. Letter from Mac in which he said he had sent my Photo and notice to the Mail so that I shall be immortalized, or at all accounts shall bloom in print; one thinks no one will recognize the man. A great fire has been raging on the Island from the neck north for the last few days. I should think it will do a vast amount of good. Mr Salmon will greatly benefit.

From the Mace family collection

I soon realised that life in Prosser's/Buckland in the 1870s and '80s was one long annual slog of farm work aligned with the seasons, and sometimes maligned by them. The backbreaking work was interspersed with natural disasters from flood to fire, and an occasional birth or death to break the monotony. On a couple of occasions Fred reports one of his farmhands as missing work in the morning due to the funeral of a child, but back at work in the afternoon. Infant fatalities were all too common, as were outbreaks of disease. Scarlet fever, diphtheria and measles made regular sweeps through the district, carrying off the young and very old.

The early diaries were written in pencil (a thick blunt one) and were particularly challenging to transcribe, although the entries were shorter and quite repetitive. While many of the individual early entries are mundane, collectively they paint a landscape of the times, of the turn of the year by the planting and harvesting of crops, the births, deaths and marriages. The compaction of a year into a couple of weeks of transcription time emphasised how hard and monotonous life must have been. No sooner had summer passed, with hay and oats cut and stooked, built into stacks and covered with "staddles" to support a thatched roof, than it was time to start ploughing and sowing for winter crops. There was little time for relaxation. Sundays flew past, with Fred either officiating as lay preacher at St John the Baptist Church, Buckland, or missing service because rain had caused the rivers to flood, leaving him stranded at home.

Many of the early diaries have large gaps in the entries, which made me wonder as to the cause. A pattern started to appear over the years. During the cold, dark winter months, Fred seemed less interested in commenting on his day. Maybe the difficulty of writing by candle or lamp light, after trying to fit a long day's work into a short one, made him lose interest. Buckland is very cold in winter, and stone houses even colder — an early bedtime would be the only way to stay warm.

Emma gave birth to five children while the Maces were at Brockley, and although she was sent to Town (Hobart) for the first three, she gave birth to two at home. She was a long way from medical help if an emergency arose. I found two newspaper clippings describing residents who had suffered a snakebite on the hand. They both immediately severed the bitten finger — their only hope for survival, as the nearest doctor was hours away and there was no antivenom. One of the diaries includes a saved clipping of a home remedy for snakebite that comprised the use of an alarming combination of gunpowder and brandy; if it didn't blow the bitten limb off you would surely be too drunk to care.

Fred's various journeys give an insight into how isolated the small towns were and how time-consuming the travel between them. The Mace's occasional family trips to Hobart were a major undertaking: horse and buggy to Campania, train to Bellerive, boat across the Derwent, then another buggy to the in-laws' home, Ferndene, in Darcy Street, South Hobart. The trip took all day, one way. If you went to town, you were gone several days. Fred speaks of locals walking to Sorell to catch the train, leaving Orford in the very early morning and covering 53 kilometres to Sorell by late afternoon.

■

By 1888, Brockley seems to have got the better of Fred. For some unspecified reason (the diary frustratingly leaves many questions unanswered), Fred and Emma moved to Malunnah, at the approach to Orford, and overlooking the bridge. They took over the property from the Meredith family, while the Buckland properties were leased out.

Wise's Tasmania Post Office Directory for 1890[2] lists 27 householders in Orford and 51 in Spring Bay (Triabunna). The road from Orford, through Paradise to Buckland and beyond, was rough and rock-strewn, and the bridges and creek crossings frequently washed out in wet weather. This treacherous road was the scene of many accidents, but was frequently travelled in the dark, and in awful weather. In early January 1900, the horse-drawn coach from Swansea, after leaving Buckland, had a brake failure on Bust-My-Gall Hill, causing the horses to "make a very fast pace downhill". The coach overturned and the driver and 17 passengers were ejected, suffering a variety of injuries. Amazingly, no one was killed. The road in the other direction, to Spring Bay and on up the coast, would have been little better, but Fred walked from Malunnah to Spring Bay and back nearly daily — a 16-kilometre round trip. If he was lucky, a passing horse and cart might pick him up, but more often, it was shank's pony. After 1900, his lay preaching frequently took him by horse and buggy north to Swansea and south to Levendale, a daunting trip on an unformed road.

At Orford, Fred had more time on his hands, and it shows in the diaries. The writing became smaller and more cramped as he struggled to fit his daily observations into notebook-sized diaries. However, his style of writing became consistent, with few days missed.

The *Letts's No. 35* is a small notebook with three days to a page and only a single line for Sunday. Each day gave little room for expansive writing, so Fred tried to give a potted summary of the events that stood out to him and included his weather observations. This led to some quite amusing *non-sequiturs*, some made worse by the lack of punctuation. In the World War I diaries, there was obvious conflict between Fred's desire to report on the headlines and war news, but still note his local observations:

> Wednesday, May 29, 1918
> 8 points of rain. Fine in the morning, rain shower midday, fine afternoon. Wind moderate NW. Glass down altogether 4/10. There was a little rain in the night, fine today on the whole though there was some rain about midday. Else left by car for Hobart for a little change and I got ready to go in to Spring Bay, but the day was too uncertain. Great Battle on the West front. Germans attack on the west front on the Aisne 35 mile front. Franco British fall back. Enemy's tremendous losses. French attacked south of Ypres. All day struggles!! This is only the beginning, in fact, perhaps the greatest offensive has not yet come. An old man with beard passed down driving a small trap.

Fred also seemed to be obsessed with commenting on the traffic. There was not much at the best of times. Through the years various horse-drawn coaches, traps and drays, the horseless Mail Car of the early 1900s, cyclists, motor-bikes — "bikists" and pedestrians, tramps and hawkers, made their way past Malunnah, either going down to Spring Bay and beyond or up to Buckland. Fred counted them — every one — and commented on who was aboard, their destination, and why they might be travelling.

This makes a fascinating resource for descendants of those east coasters researching their family histories, and the diaries are starting to reveal some neat little side stories, which will keep me occupied for years.

Although Fred appears to have a reputation in his family as bit of a no-hoper who was fond of a drink, this does a disservice to his memory. From Buckland he served as a councillor, and then warden for multiple terms on the early Spring Bay Council; became a JP, then a magistrate for the area, lay preacher and paramedic in an emergency. He was a founder of the Buckland Coal Prospecting Association and, unfortunately, of the Buckland and Spring Bay Eagle and Tiger Destruction Society.

After the move to Orford, Fred continued to serve the community as Warden, coroner, magistrate, member of the Road Trust, Agricultural Board, Board of Advice, Board of Health, Fruit Board and occasional Electoral officer.

He acted as caretaker of the elderly and infirm, Parish Councillor, lay preacher, early keeper of the Orford telephone and telegram office, and constant agitator for community improvements, including joining the committee to lobby for the construction of the East Bay Neck Canal (Dunalley).

■

He seems to have been a good man, to his family and the community, yet the diaries often give the impression Fred did not hold himself in high esteem. While the general tone is fairly formal and impersonal, every once in a while a small comment will leave me thinking, "Poor Fred, I don't think he is very happy." He certainly had his share of personal tragedy. The drowning death of his eldest son, Fred junior, in August, 1896, at the age of 18, struck him a particularly cruel blow. The man he turned to as a close confidante at the time was his council clerk, James McCluskey, to whom he wrote daily.

> Wrote to Mac a rather long letter, most of it of a private nature. Letters from Mac. One official and the other private — a very nice one.

Three months later, the "Spring Bay Disaster" occurred—a boating accident between Triabunna and Maria Island which left six local families without a breadwinner. James McCluskey was among those drowned. Despite what must have been extraordinary grief, Fred and his fellow councillors quickly established a relief fund for the widows and families, which received very generous contributions from all round the state.

Fred kept a paternal eye on residents of the district who might be struggling to get by. When "old Harry Clark" became unable to look after himself Fred personally contacted Clark's distant sons and arranged for funds to be sent to him, in trust for the old man. With the first payment, Fred took old Clark and kitted him out with a good coat, boots and blankets, then made sure he had enough funds to be going on with on a regular basis. He was a frequent visitor to the sick and elderly of Orford, Buckland and Triabunna.

■

The transcription work continues, and Fred's life and the early days of the Spring Bay region, unfold before me. Now fully tuned in to his thought patterns and with the cast of characters memorised, I find I stumble over words or names less often and have a routine going. Each day's entry has the weather conditions written at a 90-degree angle to the main text. I scan each diary so that I can rotate the view. Then, working on twin screens, I go through the daily weather report first. Then, right-side up, I go back through the diary to add each entry, adding newspaper clippings of interest, or to add clarity, and scanned letters and invoices. Mindful of my aim of making the diaries readable for Fred's great-great-grandchildren, I add footnotes to explain any unusual words or terms.

As I transcribe, I frequently become intrigued by various people and events that Fred mentions in passing, and detour to track down more information. The National Library of Australia's digitised newspapers (Trove) contain a wealth of supporting information, which has helped flesh out some of these leads. Fred had a mysterious habit of making mention of an event that one would think would require some expansion on his part, only never to refer to it again. He will sometimes discuss the aftermath without reference to the event, as if he expects the reader to know what came before. I frequently find myself muttering, "What is that all about, Fred?"

Not having the journal habit myself, I wonder why a person keeps a diary. If Fred was writing for future generations, why did he make off-hand references to momentous events giving no background or detail as if the reader should know? If he kept it only as an aide memoir, why the fascination with counting and listing passengers in the coach, and which newspapers arrived with the English mail. I can understand listing crops sown and harvested, as a statistical record, but did he really need to remember when he cleaned out the "little house" (the outside loo)? Again, I ask myself, "Who he was writing for, himself or posterity?" He listed every letter he sent, and received (and kept many of them) and every amount he paid, to whom and for what, and these details alone make the diaries a valuable historical resource.

■

As 2018 marks the 100-year anniversary of the end of World War I, on New Year's Eve 2017, again at Woodsden, the Maces and I launched Fred onto social media. His Facebook page, "Frederick Mace Esq. 100 Years to the Day", posts his corresponding diary entry from 100 years ago, each evening at 8pm, around the time he was writing it all those years ago.

At the time of writing this, I am approaching 650,000 words transcribed, with another 19 diaries to complete, plus one, the last diary of "the Mother".

I feel completely immersed in Fred's world and the history of Tasmania's east coast. Occasionally I find myself speaking in Fred's voice and my mind is full of all the surrounding stories, and future paths to follow. There is so much of the minutiae of daily life packed onto the pages that I could spend the next 20 years extracting data and stories — and probably will.

■ ■ ■

ENDNOTES

1. Advertisement, *The Mercury* (Hobart, Tas.: 1860–1954) October 7, 1870; Web. September 17, 2018, http://nla.gov.au/nla.news-article8863665.
2. *Wise's Tasmania Post Office Directory* for 1890 (Hobart: H. Wise & Co.); (London: Kelly & Co., 1891–1948). https://stors.tas.gov.au/AUTAS001126438076.

How archaeology helped save the Franklin River

Dr BILLY GRIFFITHS

On July 1, 1983, in a dramatic four-three decision, the High Court of Australia ruled to stop the damming of the Franklin River. It brought an end to a protracted campaign that had helped bring down two state premiers and a prime minister, as well as overseeing the rise of a new figure on the political landscape, the future founder of the Greens, Bob Brown.

The fact that a remote corner of south-west Tasmania became the centre of national debate reflects what was at stake in the campaigns against hydro-electric development. For many, like novelist James McQueen, the Franklin was "not just a river". "It is the epitome of all the lost forests, all the submerged lakes, all the tamed rivers, all the extinguished species".[1] The campaign was a fight for the survival of "a corner of Australia untouched by man"; it was a fight for the right of wilderness to exist.[2]

"It is a wild and wondrous thing," Brown wrote of the Franklin River in May, 1978, "and 175 years after Tasmania's first European settlement, the Franklin remains much as it was before man — black or white — came to its precincts."[3]

However, it was not only the idea of wilderness — of an ancient, pure, timeless landscape — that saved the Franklin. The archaeological research that took place during the campaign was at the heart of the High Court decision. Far from being untouched and pristine, south-west Tasmania had a deep human history. What was undoubtedly a natural wonder was also a cultural landscape.

The archaeological site at the centre of the campaign was, for a time, known by two names: Fraser Cave and kutikina. Kevin Kiernan, a caver and the first director of the Tasmanian Wilderness Society, was the first to rediscover the site. He and Greg Middleton recorded it on January 13, 1977, as part of a systematic survey of the lower and middle Gordon and Franklin rivers.

They were aware that the monolithic Hydro-Electric Commission was considering the region as the site for a dam and they were searching for something — "maybe a big whizz-bang cave" — that might save these valleys from being flooded.[4] In an attempt to raise awareness of this threatened landscape, they started a tradition of naming rock features in the south-west "after the political figures who would decide their fate".[5]

Fraser Cave was thus named after the sitting Prime Minister, Malcolm Fraser. There was also a Whitlam Cave, a Hayden Cave and a Bingham Arch. When the Tasmanian Nomenclature Board caught wind of this tradition, they accused Kiernan and other members of the Sydney Speleological Society of "gross impertinence" for naming caves outside their state.[6] In mid-1982, at the suggestion of the Tasmanian Aboriginal Centre, Fraser Cave became kutikina, which means "spirit" in the oral tradition nurtured by the dispossessed Tasmanian Aboriginal community on Babel Island in Bass Strait.[7]

Although Kiernan admired the natural splendour of kutikina in 1977, he did not recognise the artefacts it contained as human-made. It was not until he returned in February 1981 that he realised what he had found.

He and the new director of the Tasmanian Wilderness Society, Bob Brown, and its secretary, Bob Burton, were searching the remote valley for evidence of a convict who had supposedly perished in the region after escaping the Macquarie Harbour Penal Station. The story conjured the "wildness" of the country and the discovery of his bones might help bring publicity to their campaign against the dam. When they climbed through the entrance of kutikina, they were amazed to find a sea of stone artefacts and ashy hearths extending into the dark. These were no convict bones.[8]

Three weeks later, a team of archaeologists, cavers and National Parks officers rafted down the Franklin River to investigate. It was already dark on March 9, 1981, when they tied their boats to the riverbank. They had a deep chill after hours navigating the fast-flowing river, hauling their aluminium punt and rubber dingy over successive rapids, journeying deeper into the dense rainforest. The rain picked up again as they unloaded their gear and took shelter in the mouth of the cave, which opened "like a huge, curved shell".[9]

Some of the team started a small, smoky fire to cook their dinner, while the others, with the light of their torches, ventured into the cavern. kutikina opened out "like an aircraft hangar" and extended for almost 200 metres into the cliff. But it was not its scale that excited them: it was the idea that this remote cave, buried in thick "horizontal" rainforest, could have once been home to a thriving human population.[10]

Too tired to erect their tents, they unrolled their sleeping mats on the disturbed floor at the cave entrance. They were probably the first people to sleep there in about 15,000 years.

Over the following days, as rain poured outside, the team carefully surveyed kutikina. The archaeologists — Rhys Jones and Don Ranson — opened a small trench where the black sediment of the floor was covered by a thin layer of soft stalagmite. The test pit extended to a depth of only 1.2 metres before it met bedrock, but it yielded an extraordinary 75,000 artefacts and 250,000 animal bone fragments.

This small pit represented about one per cent of the artefact-bearing deposit, making the cave one of the richest archaeological sites in Australia. "In terms of the number of stone tools," Jones said to one journalist, it was "much, much richer than Mungo." [11]

The archaeological remains at kutikina told a remarkable story. The tools appeared to be a regional variant of the "Australian core tool and scraper tradition" found across the mainland during the Pleistocene, suggesting immense chains of cultural connection before the creation of Bass Strait. The bone fragments were also curious. Most had been charred or smashed to extract marrow, and 95 per cent were wallaby bones, suggesting a finely targeted hunting strategy, similar to that found in the Dordogne region in France.[12]

Most surprisingly, underneath the upper layer of hearths there were angular fragments of limestone that appeared to have shattered and fallen from the cave roof at a time of extreme cold, forming rubble on the floor. It was one of the main pieces of evidence that led Jones to speculate in his diary, "Is this the late glacial technology?" [13]

■

The possibility of Ice Age dates conjured the image of a dramatically different world. Pollen records in the region revealed that what is now rainforest was once an alpine herb field like the tundra found in Alaska, northern Russia and northern Canada. Twenty-thousand years ago, the mighty trees of ancient

Gondwanaland had retreated to the river gorges, where they were irrigated and sheltered from fire, while wallabies and wombats roamed the high, open plains above.

The cold blast of Antarctica, then only 1,000 kilometres to the south, had dropped temperatures by about 6.5 degrees Celsius. A 65-square-kilometre ice cap presided over the central Tasmanian plateau, feeding a 12-kilometre-long glacier that gripped the upper Franklin valley. Icebergs floated off the Tasmanian coast.

At the height of the last Ice Age, kutikina was home to the southern-most humans on earth. The people of south-west Tasmania hunted red-necked wallabies on the broad open slopes of Franklin valley, they collected fine stone from glacial melt water gravels and chipped them into tools, and they sheltered beside fires in the mouths of deep, limestone caverns. "They alone," Jones reflected, "may have experienced the high latitude, glacier-edge conditions of a southern Ice Age." [14]

Significantly, during a separate excavation near the confluence of the Denison and Gordon rivers, archaeologists also discovered tools and charcoal dating to 250-450 years ago, long after the ice cap had melted and the rainforest had returned.[15] It revealed that the river valleys of south-west Tasmania had a recent, as well as a deep, Aboriginal history.

■

The rediscovery of kutikina made the front page of the local and national newspapers, and was discussed on the floor of Parliament, but, surprisingly, it was restricted to the margins of the conservation campaign. John Mulvaney later reflected on the productive, albeit tense alliance between archaeologists and conservationists during the campaign. "We claimed an Ice Age environment of tundra-like grasslands, where their dearly-loved primeval forest was supposed to have stood eternally. By discrediting the image of a forest wilderness, we were ruining their image and battle cry!"[16]

Added to this tension was the animosity the Tasmanian Aboriginal community felt towards both the archaeologists, for fossicking on their land, and the conservationists, for suggesting they had never lived there. Their activism during the campaign had profound implications for the Australian archaeological community. But while Aboriginal leaders such as Rosalind Langford and Michael Mansell were eager to regain control of kutikina — "the most sacred thing in the state" — they also recognised the value of the history that had been uncovered. As Mansell said: "The fact that the Aborigines could survive physically and culturally in adverse conditions and over such a long period of time ... helps me counteract the feeling of racial inferiority and enables me to demonstrate within the wider community that I and my people are the equal of other members of the community."[17]

At the 1981 Tasmanian Power Referendum, 47 per cent of the electorate voted in favour of the Gordon-below-Franklin dam. Remarkably, there was a 45 per cent informal vote. Tens of thousands of voters had scrawled "no dams" on their ballot papers. The unprecedented "write-in" had been organised by the Tasmanian Wilderness Society, led by Brown. It repeated this highly organised, campaign-oriented strategy at local, state and federal elections throughout 1982.[18]

The federal leader of the Australian Democrats, Don Chipp, also recognised the mood of the electorate against the dam and in August, 1981, initiated a Senate inquiry into "the federal responsibility in assisting Tasmania to preserve its wilderness areas of national and international importance".[19] Jones, Mulvaney and the executive of the Australian Archaeological Association were among the many to make submissions to the new Senate Select Committee.

The Tasmanian Aboriginal Centre also made a submission, drawing upon the archaeological research to underline the cave's "great historical importance". But they also made a more personal plea. The Franklin River caves "form part of us—we are of them and they of us. Their destruction represents a part destruction of us."[20]

This advocacy had a profound influence. Several members of the Senate Committee flew into the Franklin valley to see the ongoing archaeological work, and when the committee presented its report on the "Future Demand and Supply of Electricity for Tasmania and Other Matters", the archaeology dominated the "other matters".

"Apart from any other reasons for preserving the area," they concluded, "the caves are of such importance that the Franklin River be not inundated."[21]

Prime Minister Fraser heeded the conclusions of the report. He did not want the Franklin dam built, but he was reluctant to intervene in what he regarded as a state matter. So he did not act when construction on the dam began in July 1982.[22]

On December 14, 1982, the same day the region was formally listed as a World Heritage site for its natural and cultural value, a chain of rubber rafts blocked the main landing sites along the Franklin River, protestors occupied the dam site and rallies were held in cities across Australia.²³

By autumn 1983, 1,272 protestors had been arrested during the Franklin blockade, and nearly 450 had done time in Hobart's Risdon Prison, including Mansell and Langford, who were charged with trespass on their return from visiting kutikina.²⁴

While the blockade continued, and with a federal election just around the corner, the ALP made a snap change in its leadership on February 3, 1983. It replaced Bill Hayden, who had voted at the party's national conference against Labor's policy to stop the dam, with Bob Hawke, who had voted for it. And in a tumultuous few hours of Australian political history, Fraser called an early election on the same day. It would turn out to be a grievous political miscalculation.²⁵

Neither Fraser nor Hawke believed the Franklin River dispute decided the March 5, 1983, election, but the outgoing Deputy Prime Minister, Doug Anthony, was adamant. "There is no doubt that the dam was the issue that lost the government the election,"²⁶ he said.

On March 31, the new Hawke government passed regulations to prevent further construction on the Franklin dam. Tasmanian Premier Robin Gray took the matter to the High Court, challenging the constitutionality of Hawke's "interventionist" legislation. His appeal failed by the narrowest of margins.

The judges in the majority considered that the Commonwealth had a clear obligation to use its external affairs power to stop the proposed dam, as the inundation of "the Franklin River, including kutikina Cave and Deena Reena Cave", would breach the *World Heritage Properties Conservation Act* and damage Australia's international standing. They also invoked the Commonwealth power to make laws with respect to Aboriginal people.²⁷

The Franklin River campaign has entered "the folklore of Australian environmentalism" as a green victory: a battle won, in Clive Hamilton's words, through "the intrinsic worth of wild places".²⁸ But behind the scenes it was the deep Aboriginal history of the region that pushed the decision over the line. The archaeological evidence featured in every report about the judgement, and privately Malcolm Fraser considered it to be the deciding factor.²⁹

■ ■ ■

ENDNOTES

1. James McQueen, *The Franklin: Not Just a River* (Ringwood, Vic: Penguin, 1983), 2.
2. Peter Thompson, *Bob Brown of the Franklin River* (Sydney: Allen & Unwin, 1984), 186.
3. Bob Brown as quoted in Peter Thompson, *Bob Brown of the Franklin River* (Sydney: Allen & Unwin, 1984), 94.
4. Kevin Kiernan, "Discovering the Franklin", in Roger Green (ed.), *Battle for the Franklin: Conversations with the Combatants in the Struggle for South West Tasmania* (Sydney: Fontana/Australian Conservation Foundation, 1984), 82–99, 93.
5. Kevin Kiernan, "Days in a Wilderness", *Southern Caver* 12(4) (May 1981), 72–78, 77.
6. Tim Bonyhady, "So much for a name" in Tim Bonyhady and Tom Griffiths (eds.), *Words for Country: Landscape & Language in Australia* (Sydney: University of New South Wales Press, 2001), 140–161.
7. The full story behind the name is told in Jim Everett, "Tasmania", in Oodgeroo Noonuccal (ed.), *Australian Legends and Landscapes* (Milsons Point, NSW: Random House, 1990), 100–125, 121–125.
8. Kiernan, "Days in a Wilderness", 75.
9. Rhys Jones and Kenneth Russell Henderson, "The Extreme Climatic Place? An Interview with Rhys Jones", *Hemisphere* 26(1) (Jul/Aug 1981), 54–59, 56.
10. Rhys Jones, "Trip to Franklin River", Field Journals, AIATSIS, Canberra, MS 5040/1/50, March 9, 1981.
11. Jones and Henderson, "The Extreme Climatic Place?", 55.
12. Rhys Jones, "Submission to the Senate Select Committee on South West Tasmania", Commonwealth Hansard, March 19, 1982, 1715–1764, as reprinted in *Australian Archaeology* 14 (1982) 96–106, 101.
13. Jones, "Field Journals, Trip to Franklin River, S.W. Tasmania", March 12, 1981.
14. Rhys Jones, "From Kakadu to Kutikina: The Southern Continent at 18,000 Years Ago", in Olga Soffer and Clive Gamble (eds.), *The World at 18,000 BP* (London: Unwin Hyman, 1990), 264–295, 290–291.
15. Jones initially claimed the find to be of Pleistocene antiquity. Jones, "Submission to the Senate Select Committee on South West Tasmania", 99.
16. John Mulvaney, *Digging up a Past* (Sydney: UNSW Press, 2011), 238.
17. Mansell as quoted in Lyndall Ryan, *Tasmanian Aborigines: A History since 1803* (Sydney: Allen & Unwin, 2012), 319.
18. Drew Hutton and Libby Connors, *A History of the Australian Environment Movement* (Cambridge: Cambridge University Press, 1999), 161–162.
19. Don Chipp, "Select Committee on South West Tasmania", *Senate Hansard*, August 19, 1981, 44.
20. Tasmanian Aboriginal Centre, "Submission to the Senate Select Committee on South West Tasmania, 8 February 1982", *Pugganna News* 12 (March 1982), [no page numbers].

21. Senate Select Committee on South West Tasmania, *Future Demand and Supply of Electricity for Tasmania and Other Matters* (Canberra: Australian Government Publishing Service, November 1982), 204.
22. Malcolm Fraser and Margaret Simons, *Malcolm Fraser: The Political Memoirs* (Melbourne: Melbourne University Press, 2015), 580.
23. Thompson, *Bob Brown of the Franklin River*, 162–66.
24. McQueen, *The Franklin,* 43.
25. Patrick Weller, "The Anatomy of a Grievous Miscalculation: 3 February 1983", in Howard R Penniman (ed.), *Australia at the Polls: The National Elections of 1980 and 1983* (Sydney: Allen & Unwin, 1983), 248–280, 264.
26. Doug Anthony, as quoted in Thompson, *Bob Brown of the Franklin River*, 178.
27. Verge Blunden, "What the High Court Justices had to Say", *Sydney Morning Herald*, July 2, 1983, 7, 19.
28. Clive Hamilton, *What Do We Want? The Story of Protest in Australia* (Canberra: NLA Publishing, 2016), 170, 176.
29. Robyn Williams, "Down the Franklin by Lawn Mower", *Australian Archaeology* 20 (1985), 151.

The passing of the "tigerman"

NIC HAYGARTH

In 1889 the Van Diemen's Land Company (VDL Co.) advertised for "a trustworthy man to snare tigers [thylacines], kangaroo, wallaby and other vermin at Woolnorth", its primary wool pasture at Tasmania's north-western tip. The annual wage offered was £30 plus rations and a £1 bounty for each thylacine killed.[1] Written applications for the job, unofficially known as the "tigerman", came from as far afield as Branxholm and New Norfolk.

What was a "tigerman"? The term had been coined by Woolnorth overseer James Wilson to describe the position of the Mount Cameron West shepherd on that property. Convinced that thylacines were killing their sheep, the VDL Co. gave the remote Mount Cameron West man the additional job of maintaining a line of tiger snares across a narrow neck of land which was believed to be the predator's principal access point to Woolnorth. Otherwise, the "tigermen" were standard stockmen-hunters, charged with guarding sheep and destroying competitors for the grass.

Applicants took up the "tigerman" challenge. Henry Ricke of Waratah claimed to have cleared a sheep run at Bridgewater of "wild Dogs, Tigers, Devils, Hawks and other vermin".[2] John Riley of Connorville had "some experience of hunting tigers in the lake country".[3] John Denmen of Latrobe boasted five years' experience in snaring "tigers and other vermin".[4] William Beswick of Launceston had been getting £2 per tiger on Mr Baker's run "owing to them being so hard to catch".[5] Richard Hodgetts of Cressy had had "some experience tiger snaring on the Western Tiers".[6] J. Everett of Lisle proposed working for rations and £1 per tiger, but no salary, being "confident that I will easily make up for that loss. I am sure if the animals are so numerous as I have been informed

I will trap 500 per week".[7] Approaches, questions and literacy standards varied, with the apologetic John Burke of Launceston requesting "the full Per Ticklers [sic]" of the vacancy.[8]

GEORGE WAINWRIGHT (1864–1903)

None of these applicants got the job. In fact the man chosen as "tigerman" in 1889 did not submit an application — and not because of illiteracy. His assumed name, George Wilson, appeared only as a pencilled footnote on one of the written applications.[9] It was later said that he arrived at Woolnorth "under a cloud", and it seems that he was in hiding.[10] Perhaps adopting the surname of the Woolnorth overseer was part of a disguise, but it is also possible that he regarded himself as James Wilson's protégé, that the overseer had intervened to secure him the job. Someone was looking for him — and someone was looking after him!

The new "tigerman"'s real name was George Wainwright. He was born in Launceston, and seems to have had a not untypical upbringing for the poorly educated child of an ex-convict father, featuring family breakdown, petty crime, shiftlessness and suggestions of poverty.[11] Even as a young adult he measured only 162 cm (5'3" inches), with a dark complexion and dark curly hair. The scar under his chin may have been the result of rough times on the streets of Launceston.[12] Food may have been scarce. At 13 he and another boy were charged with stealing apples (the case was dismissed for lack of evidence).[13] In 1883, his employer, Launceston butcher Richard Powell, had the 19-year-old arrested on warrant (that is, *in absentia*) on a charge of breaching the *Master and Servant Act*.[14] He had run off to Sydney, describing himself as a cook.[15]

George had returned to Launceston by October of that year, when his mother ran a public notice instructing clergymen not to marry her under-age son to anyone.[16] Presumably George had Matilda Maria Carey (1863-1941) — or her pregnancy — in mind, because the couple were soon united, and soon separated.[17] In 1885 Matilda prosecuted George for deserting her and George junior, he having not sent her any money for six months. It was revealed in court in Melbourne that George was now working in a Brunswick (Melbourne) brick yard. He was freed on agreeing to pay her 10 shillings per week.[18]

In Victoria George Wainwright was known to police as George Brown, "alias Wainwright".[19] He returned to Launceston — and changed his name to George Wilson. He may have been the George Wilson who was in Beaconsfield in 1886 and 1887.[20] Perhaps he had already become the protégé of James Wilson, the Woolnorth overseer, and perhaps that intervention secured Wainwright/Brown/Wilson the Mount Cameron West job at Woolnorth.

■

So a tiny man became the "tigerman". From this distance it's hard to imagine 25-year-old delinquent George Wainwright filling the shoes of someone called the "tigerman". The term conjures up visions of tiger hunts in the British Raj, of man-eating Bengal tigers hoisted as trophies by a pith-helmeted, safari-suited, broad-seated British trader with a blunderbuss, a team of beaters and a yearning to fill the empty mount between the tusked elephant and rhino heads on his smoking room wall.

The reality at Woolnorth was quite different. While the VDL Co. was a British Colonial enterprise granted land under royal charter, Woolnorth was not the jewel in anyone's crown. The company tried for decades to offload it.[21] The property, which only became the VDL Co.'s primary wool pasture by default, was kept in a run-down state in order to minimise spending ahead of its disposal.[22]

Nor did the Tasmanian "tiger" measure up to the Indian man-eater. "Tiger" and "tigerman" were equally unintimidating. A recent scientific study has suggested that the jaws of the *Thylacinus cynocephalus*, the timid, endemic Tasmanian marsupial, were not strong enough for sheep consumption, adding weight to the belief that for 19th-century Tasmanian wool-growers the thylacine was more scapegoat than predator.[23] The names "tiger" and "hyena" were commonly used to describe the thylacine, with "tiger" becoming easily the dominant term in the late 19th century (see Table 1). The Bengal tiger (*Panthera tigris tigris*) and the striped hyena (*Hyaena hyaena*) were mentioned regularly in Tasmanian newspaper accounts of life in the British Raj.

Tigers, leopards, cheetahs, wolves and, less often, hyenas preyed on stock and sometimes people in India. Government rewards were offered there for killing tigers. While the fearsome tiger was the favourite "sport" of Indian big game hunters, the hyena, unlike its some-time Tasmanian namesake, was not the primary carnivore in the subcontinental ecology. It was sometimes reported to be "cowardly", "skulking" and lacking in the fight desired by the game hunter.[24]

Table 1: Occurrences of various names for the thylacine in Tasmanian newspapers 1816-1954 (in both text and advertising), taken from the Trove digital newspaper database 24 September 2018.

NAME	1816-87	1888-1909	1910-54	TOTAL
Tasmanian tiger	121 (72–49)	177 (99–78)	656 (561–95)	954 (732–222)
Dog-tiger	1 (1–0)	0 (0–0)	0 (0–0)	1 (1–0)
Native tiger	369 (217–152)	321 (282–39)	130 (129–1)	820 (628–192)
Thylacinus/ *Thylacinus cynocephalus*	37 (37–0)	14 (14–0)	31 (30–1)	82 (81–1)
Thylacine	9 (9–0)	14 (14–0)	105 (100–5)	128 (123–5)
Hyena/ native hyena/ opossum hyena	176 (106–70)	49 (35–14)	129 (85–44)	354 (226–128)
Dog-faced opossum	1 (1–0)	0 (0–0)	0 (0–0)	1 (1–0)
Tasmanian wolf	10 (4–6)	15 (14–1)	107 (107–0)	132 (125–7)
Marsupial wolf	4 (4–0)	12 (12–0)	79 (78–1)	95 (94–1)
Tiger wolf	7 (7–0)	4 (4–0)	5 (5–0)	16 (16–0)
Native wolf/ native wolf-dog	5 (5–0)	0 (0–0)	7 (7–0)	12 (12–0)
Zebra wolf/ Tasmanian zebra wolf	5 (5–0)	7 (7–0)	3 (3–0)	15 (15–0)
Tasmanian tiger wolf	2 (2–0)	0 (0–0)	1 (1–0)	3 (3–0)[25]

Likewise, the thylacine was also often described as "cowardly" in its alleged sheep predations.[26] By the 1870s and 1880s, however, when the profitability of the wool industry was declining, those employed in the industry seem to have used the term "tiger" almost universally to describe the thylacine. This re-branding of the thylacine was a major step in stigmatising it as a sheep killer. Perhaps shepherds preferred "tiger" because it glamorised their profession, introducing an element of danger and likening them to the big game hunters of India. The way in which some thylacine killers made trophies of their kills and were photographed with these suggests identification with big game hunting.[27]

Dubbing the thylacine a "tiger" also provided a potential scapegoat for sheep losses, enabling the shepherd to shift the blame for his own poor performance on to what may henceforth be perceived as a dangerous predator. Wool-growers wanting to eliminate the thylacine would also be keen to cast it as a dangerous predator. John Lyne, the east coast wool-grower who led the campaign for a government thylacine bounty, referred to the animal as a "tiger" but also as a "dingo", thereby equating the thylacine with the well-known mainland Australian sheep predator.[28] In 1887 Lyne's campaign was mocked to the effect that, "The jungles of India do not furnish anything like the terrors that our own east coast does in the matter of wild beasts of the most ferocious kind. According to 'Tiger Lyne', these dreadful animals [thylacines] may be seen in their hundreds stealthily sneaking along, seeking whom they may devour …" [29]

■

Woolnorth was an isolated settlement with challenges faced by few wool-growing properties. Distance from towns, doctors and schools was probably one reason that it was so difficult to find and keep a reliable man to work at Woolnorth's most remote run, Mount Cameron West. The term "tigerman", which carried the implication of being a dedicated thylacine killer, may have been coined to glamorise the position in order to attract staff. It and the general use of the term "tiger" at Woolnorth may also indicate that the overseer, his stockmen and farm hands wanted to shift the blame for sheep losses on the property.

George "Wilson" and his family originally occupied an unglamorous, one-room hut at Mount Cameron West. One of their sons boarded with the state school teacher at Montagu so that he could receive an education.[30] Tigers probably helped pay for it. In 1893 George Wainwright, as he was now known again, apparently told a visitor that he received £2 10s for each thylacine killed — £1 from the VDL Co., £1 from the government and 10 shillings for the skin. Harry Wainwright, one of George's sons, recalled tigers caught in his father's hemp necker snares dragging the device for about ten yards before being strangled. The animals were then skinned and the heads boiled clean of meat for application for the bounty payment.[31] However, Wainwright's

George and Matilda Wainwright, centre, at Mount Cameron, c.1900.
Courtesy Kath Medwin

biggest money spinner would have been his income from hunting other native animals for their skins. In 1893, for example, he set about 60 springer snares for wallaby, pademelon and brush possum.[32]

By the mid-1890s a living tiger was also more valuable than a dead one. In June 1896 Wainwright captured a live juvenile thylacine intended for the American tour of Fitzgerald's Circus. First he shipped it to Stanley, where its arrival caused "a little excitement".[33] While it awaited trans-shipment to Sydney, stress on the poor young animal was increased by the placement of a tomcat inside its cage in hope of inducing a fight to the death.[34] The thylacine survived this ordeal and the voyage. Who was more wide-eyed — audience or thylacine — when, three weeks later, it toured northern Queensland as part of Fitzgerald's "ENORMOUS Wild Animal Exhibition"?[35] Presumably the thylacine died in its enclosure, like its zoo-bound counterparts.

In 1897-98 a new hut was built for George and Matilda at Mount Cameron West. They would need it. Seven children — George, Alf, Dick, May, Harry, Gertrude and Robert (Bob) — gave them plenty to worry about in such an isolated place. Matilda survived severe illness and injury here, with medicine having to be fetched for her by ship from Stanley.[36] She also survived the nerve-wracking experience of giving birth at the Mount Cameron West hut with only the help of a midwife. So entrenched was the tiger in her son Harry's childhood that he mistook the wail of the newborn for the animal's cry.[37]

VDL Co. records suggest that George Wainwright senior's biggest yearly haul was 16 in 1900, and that his total kill was 55. The boys also went after their own tigers.[38] More importantly, however, they learned how to dig potatoes.[39] With their father sometimes helping out elsewhere on the property, fetching cattle from Ridgley or a stockman from Trefoil Island, the Wainwright children quickly developed a range of skills which ensured that they could work on the land independently.[40]

■

George Wainwright's imprisonment in 1903 forced them to test that independence. He was convicted of receiving stolen skins: 298 wallaby, 298 pademelon, 17 tiger cat, two domestic cat and ten brush possum.[41] Perhaps previous indiscretions counted against him, because he was sentenced to 12 months' gaol.[42] Thirty-nine years old, George Wainwright died in the Hobart Gaol of heart failure prompted by acute pneumonia only four months into that sentence.[43]

Like the tiger he sent to the circus, he died in a cage. Today a relatively young man's death in custody would provoke not just an inquest but parliamentary and public debate. However, the harshness of Wainwright's demise seems in keeping with the harshness of his sentence and the general torpor of working people's lives more than a century ago.

"Tigerman" and "tiger" shared a common fate. The Woolnorth tiger snares became redundant, as the thylacine became critically endangered. Thus was fractured an unlikely tableau of hunter and predator on a far-flung pasture at the edge of the empire.

■ ■ ■

ENDNOTES

1. "Wanted, at Woolnorth", *Daily Telegraph*, August 9, 1889, 1.
2. Henry Ricke to James Norton Smith August 10, 1889, VDL22/1/19 (Tasmanian Archive and Heritage Office, afterwards TAHO).
3. John Riley to James Norton Smith August 13, 1889, VDL22/1/19 (TAHO).

4. John Denmen to James Norton Smith August 13, 1889, VDL22/1/19 (TAHO).
5. William Beswick to James Norton Smith, undated, VDL22/1/19 (TAHO).
6. Richard Hodgetts to James Norton Smith August 12, 1889, VDL22/1/19 (TAHO).
7. J. Everett to James Norton Smith, 19 August, 1889, VDL22/1/19 (TAHO).
8. John Burke to James Norton Smith 12 August, 1889, VDL22/1/19 (TAHO).
9. "Geo Wilson also". See J Lowe to James Norton Smith, August 9, 1889, VDL22/1/19 (TAHO).
10. A. K. McGaw, Outward Despatch, no. 16, June 1, 1903, 151, VDL7/1/13 (TAHO).
11. For William Wainwright (1810–1887), see conduct record, CON33-1-90 (TAHO), http://search.archives.tas.gov.au/ImageViewer/image_viewer.htm?CON33-1-90,207,205,F,60.
12. "Miscellaneous Information", *Victoria Police Gazette*, August 19, 1885, 232.
13. Birth registration 60/1864, Launceston (TAHO); "Police Court", *Cornwall Chronicle*, February 7, 1877, 3.
14. "Launceston Police Court", *Tasmanian*, April 22, 1882, 432; "Launceston Police Court", *Launceston Examiner*, February 7, 1883, 3.
15. He arrived in Sydney from Launceston on the *Esk*, February 9, 1883, New South Wales, Australia, Unassisted Passenger Lists, 1826–1922 (TAHO).
16. Advertisement, *Launceston Examiner*, October 31, 1883, 1.
17. Matilda Maria Carey was born in Launceston, 22 December 1863, birth registration 23/1864. They married in Launceston, November 7, 1883, marriage registration 677/1883. George William Wainwright was born in Launceston, June 12, 1884, birth registration 371/1884 (TAHO).
18. "Wife Desertion", *Launceston Examiner*, August 29, 1885, 2.
19. "Miscellaneous Information", *Victoria Police Gazette*, August 19, 1885, 232.
20. "Beaconsfield", *Daily Telegraph*, May 29, 1886, 3; "Beaconsfield", *Launceston Examiner*, January 15, 1887, 12.
21. Woolnorth was tenanted 1852–1871, but otherwise the VDL Co. could not find a tenant willing to take it.
22. For the comparatively disastrous early sheep grazing at the Hampshire and Surrey Hills, see V.D.L. Co. Court of Directors to Edward Curr, February 26, 1835, Inward Despatch 126, VDL193/1/3 (TAHO).
23. For weak jaws, see M. R. G. Attard, U. Chamoli, T. L. Ferrara, T. L .Rogers and S. Wroe, "Skull Mechanics and Implications for Feeding Behaviour in a Large Marsupial Carnivore Guild: the Thylacine, Tasmanian Devil and Spotted-tailed Quoll", *Journal of Zoology* 285 (2011), 292–300. For the thylacine as a scapegoat, see Robert Paddle, *The Last Tasmanian Tiger: the history and extinction of the thylacine*, (Cambridge, UK: Cambridge University Press, 2000), 98–138.
24. "Pigsticking in India", *Launceston Examiner,* March 29, 1897, 3; "Shikalee"; "Wild Sport in India", *Launceston Examiner,* July 24, 1897, 2.
25. The numbers in brackets indicate how many of the hits occurred in text and how many in advertising respectively. The second period defined, 1888–1909, corresponds to the years of the Tasmanian government thylacine bounty (£1 for an adult thylacine carcass and 10 shillings for a juvenile).

26. See, for example, "Royal Society of Tasmania", *Courier,* June 16, 1858, 2; or "Town Talk and Table Chat", *Cornwall Chronicle,* March 27, 1867, 4.
27. See, for example, [Theophilus Jones], "Through Tasmania: no.35", *Mercury,* April 26, 1884, supplement, 1.
28. See, for example, "Parliament", *Launceston Examiner,* October 1, 1886, 3.
29. *Tasmanian Mail,* September 3, 1887; cited by Robert Paddle, *The Last Tasmanian Tiger,* 161.
30. J C Fitzpatrick to James Norton Smith, September 9, 1893, VDL22/1/23 (TAHO).
31. Harry Wainwright, transcript of interview by James Malley and Bob Brown at Smithton, October 1, 1972 (QVMAG).
32. Austin Allom, "A Trip to the West Coast", *Daily Telegraph,* August 19, 1893, 7.
33. "Circular Head Notes", *Wellington Times and Agricultural and Mining Gazette,* June 25, 1896, 2.
34. "The Tiger and the Cat", *Wellington Times and Agricultural and Mining Gazette,* July 2, 1896, 2.
35. Advertisement, *Daily Northern Argus* (Rockhampton), July 20, 1896, 2.
36. Woolnorth Farm Journal, July 10, 1893, VDL277/1/20; January 22, 1894, VDL277/1/21; and May 7 1900, VDL277/1/25 (TAHO).
37. Harry Wainwright, transcript of interview, December 10, 1970 (QVMAG).
38. Woolnorth Farm Journal, June 13 and 14, 1900, VDL277/1/25 (TAHO).
39. Woolnorth Farm Journal, May 7, 1900, VDL277/1/25 (TAHO).
40. Woolnorth Farm Journal, September 22, 1898, VDL277/1/24; January 16 and March 5, 1899, VDL277/1/25 (TAHO).
41. "Supreme Court", *Mercury,* November 15, 1902, 3; "The Wainwright Case", *Examiner,* February 28, 1903, 6.
42. "The Wainwright Case", *Examiner,* February 27, 1903, 6.
43. Inquest no.11584, July 14 1903, SC195-1-75-11584 (TAHO), https://librariestas.ent.sirsidynix.net.au/client/en_AU/names/search/results?qu=george&qu=wainwright, accessed September 22, 2018. George left Matilda £305 ("Testamentary", *Mercury,* October 20, 1903, 4), more than ten times his annual wage.

Constitution Dock: construction, naming and tragedies

TERRY NEWMAN

The best-known area of the Port of Hobart is Constitution Dock, not least because since 1948 it has been the destination for many of the boats completing the Sydney to Hobart Yacht Race. More recently, it has seen other events, including the biennial Wooden Boat Festival. But little is known of the dock's origins, therefore this history presents construction details and some early dock modifications. Also coincidental incidents are mentioned, especially the dock's naming, which relates to Tasmania's system of government and accompanying celebrations.

While the dock's facilities are ever evolving, its original function can be said to begin with the widening of the causeway to Hunter's Island, which took place between 1816 and 1826.[1] By 1901 the *Cyclopedia of Tasmania* noted that "Sullivan's Cove [is] the principal anchorage of Hobart ... Here all the shipping business of the city is conducted, and at times this is of considerable magnitude."[2]

■

The history of Constitution Dock began with Lt-Governor William Denison, who started his career as a military engineer before administering the government of Tasmania (1846–1855). Before Tasmania, Denison's civil projects included to "superintend dockyard and similar works at Woolwich, Portsmouth and Bermuda". He also undertook a project similar to Hobart's dock when, in 1841, he was "called upon to draw plans and estimates for a harbour of refuge at Devon."[3]

In Tasmania, Denison drew upon this experience and even presented a pertinent talk at the Royal Society of Van Diemen's Land (renamed Tasmania January 1856). In July, 1849, Denison wrote "On docks; dry, wet, and floating".[4] Linking previous projects to Hobart, he wrote that the "limestone of Maria Island is found to yield a lime which sets under water as hard as Roman cement, and [it] engineered the entrance of Constitution Dock".[5] Given the date of Denison's paper it is clear that work on the dock had already commenced. In fact, its design had been prepared by Government Works director William Porden Kay, who sadly had an accident — described below — on his way home from the dock's official opening.

An early description of the immediate area of the dock appeared in the *Cyclopedia of Tasmania*, which described the surrounding waterfront: "The whole of the ground from Customs Bonded Stores [today's TMAG] at the corner of Davey Street, to the Constitution Dock, was, as old colonialists will recollect, simply a beach."[6] This beach was, of course, before Davey Street was extended in 1862 from Elizabeth Street towards the Queen's Domain.

But, as hinted at by Denison, work on the dock actually started in mid-May, 1848. On May 12, the *Colonial Times* reported that a "gang of able-bodied men arrived from Port Arthur to be placed under sufficient superintendence upon this public work". These men "commenced operations with vigour and ability", and that the "work in progress (is) deserving of all commendation".[7] At the same time the *Courier* reported on "The Wharves":

> It is proposed to complete the Franklin Wharf as originally intended, except that the basin next Argyle-street, instead of being filled up, will be converted into a boat harbour.[8]

A glowing report also appeared in the *Hobart Guardian* :

> These improvements, carried into effect, there will scarcely be in the world a more perfect harbour than ours. Of easy access, and replete with every possible accommodation.[9]

However, just over a year after work commenced on July 20, 1849, an inquest was held for a man named Daniel Whiston:

> ... who met his death, by falling accidentally on Friday night at twelve o'clock, from the platform erected for the purposes of pumping out water at the place where the new dock is in the course of construction.

It appears that the poor man, in his hurry to leave his work for the purposes of getting his midnight meal, missed his footing and fell into the dock, and in his fall struck his head against the side and fractured his skull; he was immediately conveyed to her Majesty's general hospital, where he expired.[10]

Whiston, a collier from Macclesfield, England had been tried at Liverpool for burglary in March, 1843, and arrived in Tasmania aboard the *Sir George Seymour* in February, 1845, aged 21. His convi"out of hours on the Cascade Road with implements for picking locks in his coat" and so his ticket-of-leave was revoked, hence his presence on the dock's labour gang. The inquest was held at the *Brunswick Wine Vaults* (Liverpool Street), and "Dr [James Wilson] Agnew — a future Tasmanian Premier — described the nature of the injuries and the jury returned a verdict of accidental death."[11]

Shortly after this tragic accident, in August, 1849, Works Director W. P. Kay gave a report to Parliament on the "New Wharf at Hobart Town", which dealt with the Franklin Wharf and the dock described as the "new basin".[12] Kay noted that to deepen the dock some 25,500 cubic yards of rock had been taken from it to form the "embankment" of the new wharf. This meant, he wrote, that the depth of the dock would achieve "9 feet at dead low water of spring tides". By October, 1850, another parliamentary report described the "new basin" as "advanced", and the press was able to say that "we understand that the New Dock, at Franklin Wharf, is expected to be finished by 1st December next."[13]

Upon completion, the formal opening of the dock took place at the 13th Hobart Regatta on December 3, 1850. Perhaps the regatta's number was unlucky because the weather that day was described as "disagreeable and disastrous". Apperently, the "morning was fine, but towards 12 o'clock the whirlwinds of dust accompanied by occasional showers of rain rendered it almost impossible to see the races" taking place on the Derwent.[14] Nevertheless, the *Courier* reported on the new dock with some precision, noting that is was "320 feet long, 270 feet wide and 18 feet deep" at high tide.

As always, it was argued that the dock could have been built better and cheaper, but concerning its name, local merchants had sought to flatter the Lt-Governor by suggesting that it be named Denison Dock. But instead he suggested the current name because a pivotal event in Tasmania's history had overtaken this sycophancy. Although Denison did agree that the next dock would bear his name — except that it was subsequently named Fisherman's Dock.[15]

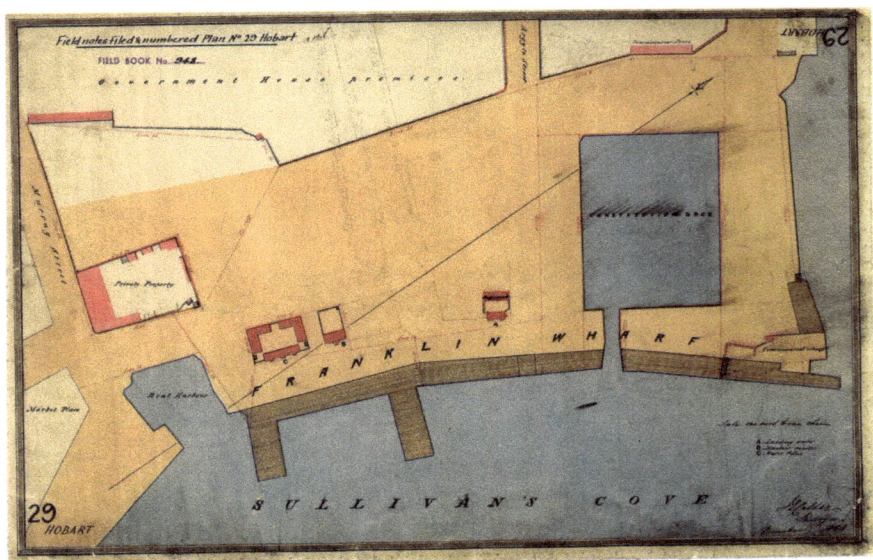

Hobart Map 29: Plan of Franklin Wharf and Constitution Dock.
Surveyor: James Erskine Calder.
Source: Libraries Tasmania: http://Stors.tas.gov.au/AF394_1_27

The recent event Denison referred to was reported on by the *Courier*. It described "rejoicing" on November 20, 1850, when news reached Hobart of the *Act for the Better Government of Her Majesty's Australian Colonies*. Elsewhere, the *Hobart Town Advertiser* had it that the locals were now on "alert" because this legislation meant that they were about to gain the right to create self-government for Tasmania. So Constitution Dock's name marks Tasmania's first steps towards elective parliamentary democracy.

Meantime, at the start of the regatta, a prominent merchant Thomas Daniel Chapman (another future Premier) officially named the area "Constitution Dock". He did so amid three cheers and then Governor Denison "sailed from the steps amid the cheers of the assembled spectators who lined the margin of the dock in considerable numbers. The aquatic cortege was (then) towed to Pavilion Point by a number of "native youths", namely Europeans born in Tasmania." [16]

When W. P. Kay eventually left the regatta, he unfortunately added another dock-related incident. The *Launceston Examiner* reported,

> Proceeding home in his gig ... his horse took fright, and the vehicle coming into collision with a butcher's shop. Mr Kay's head was

struck by the iron suspending an awning in front of the window, the force of the blow bending the iron and disfiguring the unfortunate gentleman's face in a frightful manner, his nose and lower part of his jaw severely injured.[17]

Sadly, nothing further was reported on Kay's recovery, which obviously occurred because he continued his public works duties. However, the *Examiner* went on to report that the "unlucky" Regatta also featured a tragic event,

> We regret to state that a serious accident threw a damp upon the proceedings of the day. One of the sailing heats, the *British Queen*, of ten tons, whilst making her last tack, suddenly capsized and sank. Her crew, consisted of eight men, one of whom swam ashore, a second [Mr Petchey, the owner] was picked up in an exhausted state, and the remaining six were drowned.

As for the British Queen, a plaque exists today as a memorial to the sad incident on the border of Constitution Dock.[18]

■

While the arrival of constitutional news in November 1850 was the reason for the dock's name, the documentary proof establishing today's Tasmanian Parliament finally arrived in Hobart on January 31, 1851. That day the 200-ton barque *Olinda* arrived with "general cargo", which included the new Constitution in parchment form. Public rejoicing of the new political status ocurred throughout the island and Denison declared an entire week of celebrations. Indeed, budget documents record £6 13s was spent for "gunpowder on swearing in his Excellency under the new Constitution".[19] That is, a ceremonial salute of cannon was given and Denison gave a speech entitled "Success to Van Diemen's Land under its free institution".[20]

In Hobart a "Demonstration Committee" was formed at the Victoria Hotel to organise constitutional celebrations which took place on February 12 and 13, 1851. They included a games of "cricket, throwing the hammer, and pigs with soaped tails". Lady Denison's diary records that the streets were "prettily illuminated", and that fireworks rounded out each night, which her children stayed awake to watch. A new Electoral Act was also passed locally to accompany the new Constitution and, in common with that era, within days local citizens published requests for parliamentary candidates to accept nomination for the island's inaugural elections.

Regarding the dock itself, shortly after it's formal opening it was praised by a group of "ship-owners and ship-masters of vessels lying in Constitution Dock". Signed by a dozen prominent merchants, they wrote to Denison:

> We beg leave to acknowledge our sense of the benefit conferred on the colonial traders in the construction of this useful work; and to return you our thanks for the accommodation thus afforded us, which, by the increased facility for loading and unloading, is the highest degree convenient, economical, and secure.[21]

However, by the time of his departure in 1856 to become Governor of NSW, Denison's standing in Tasmania had declined because his rejection of the popular anti-convict struggle was based on his belief that without their labour Tasmania's economy would suffer (which it did).[22] Even so, the press was willing to concede to Denison some respect. Under the heading Improvements on the Wharf, it was reported,

> We were greatly struck some days ago by the improvements effected by his Excellency Sir William Denison on the New Wharf. In the course of time, the harbour of Hobart Town will be one of the best in the world. In this respect. Sir William Denison has done his duty as the Lieutenant-Governor of Van Diemen's Land, and deserves the thanks of the community. Differing from him as we do respecting the subject of the continuance of the transportation of prisoners to this island, we are honour bound by a sense of public duty to render honor to whom honor is due.[23]

In January 1858 the *Mercury* provided a "faithful description" of the accommodation for shipping, "Constructed under the superintendence of Sir Wm. Denison, and capable of containing twenty vessels of a burthen carrying from 100 to 200 tons. This dock has accommodation for berthing ten vessels alongside its wharves, and has also seven stage berths."[24]

Other positive descriptions of the early purpose for Constitution Dock suggest that it afforded "ample space for river and coastal craft, who have every facility for loading and discharging cargo in absolutely still water"[25] However, given the type of building material available in that era, it seems that by July

1855 the dock was already in need of "reconstruction".[26] The newly incumbent Governor Henry Fox Young advised the Parliament that the Director of Public Works, J. S. Hampton, "reports that the timber piles used are under going ('gradual but sure') decay from the worm, and all that are done in the last ten years will require to be renewed in the next ten".

Even before this, significant modifications of the dock were soon needed. For example, it became obvious that it would be convenient to travel directly across the face of the waterfront, and so in March 1851 the first bridge across the entrance was built by "Mr Ross at a cost of £40". Many replacement bridges have followed, and on July 2, 1858, "Mr Kelly was offered a permanent appointment at £75 per annum to operate the new swing bridge." Ross again won this tender — at £143 — and this bridge saved people from taking a "circuitous walk over the very unpleasent gravelled road around the dock."[27] It is speculated that this "Mr Kelly" was James Kelly, of colonial fame and namesake for Kelly's Steps, who died aged 68 soon after this appointment in 1859 for it was "likely [he had] ... needed an easier job".[28]

In 1864 the Hobart Marine Board employed a "Mr Watson as superintendent of works and the [dock's] entrance was rebuilt".[29]

James Kelly's change of work from sealer to bridge-operator reflects the changing functions of Constitution Dock. In 1901 the *Cyclopedia of Tasmania* described this transformation. "It served its purpose well until vessels of deeper draught were placed on the trade, and these had, of course, to be berthed elsewhere."[30] Fishing boats (and now food pontoons) have long used the dock, but just after World War Two, a rather shocking twist almost took place. With cars becoming more prevalent, a Hobart City Councillor proposed that the dock be filled in and a "three-floored carpark" be built.[31] This sacrilige was thankfully dodged, but the rise of containerised shipping has seen cargo handling at the dock relocated yet again. Finally, while the original purpose of Constitution Dock has long passed from loading and unloading, its name will forever remain attached to a landmark of the island's political history.

■ ■ ■

ENDNOTES

1. Des Wolfe, "Fisherman's dock has a long and interesting history", *Fintas*.8, no.3 (September 1985): 35–41; and Audrey Hudspeth and Linda Scripps *Capital Port: a history of the Marine Board of Hobart 1858–1997* (Hobart: Hobart Ports Corporation, 2000).
2. *The Cyclopedia of Tasmania (illustrated): an historical and commercial review: descriptive and biographical, facts, figures and illustrations: an epitome of progress: business men and commercial interests* (Launceston: Prestige Bookbinders, 1988), 1: 197.
3. Douglas Pike, Bede Nairn and Geoffrey Serle, *Australian Dictionary of Biography* (Melbourne: Melbourne Univeristy Press, 1966) http://adb.anu.edu.au/biography/denison-sir-william-thomas-3394; John Micheal Bennett, *Reluctant Democrat: Sir William Denison in Australia 1847–1861,* (Melbourne: Federation Press, 2011): 4–70.
4. William Denison, "On docks; dry, wet, and floating", *Papers & Proceedings of the Royal Society of Van Diemen's Land*, 1 part III (1851): 198–209.
5. *Hobart Town Courier,* May 24, 1851, 2.
6. *Cyclopedia of Tasmania*, I: 200.
7. *Colonial Times,* May 12, 1848, 3.
8. *Hobart Town Courier,* May 10, 1848, 2.
9. *Hobart Guardian,* May 13, 1848, 2.
10. *Colonial Times,* July 24, 1849, 3; and December 20, 1850, 2; December 27, 1850, 2. [NB: crew named in *Courier*, December 7, 1850, 3.]
11. "Names Index" State Library Tasmania references: SC195/1/25 Inquest 2113, Death RGD 34/1/2/No 1784, Convict record 1353, Archives Office Item Con-33-1-64:168.
12. "New Wharf at Hobart Town", Tasmanian Parliamentary Paper no.13/1849.
13. *Colonial Times,* October 4, 1850, 2; Tasmanian Parliamentary Paper no. 72/1852: 30.
14. *Colonial Times,* December 6, 1850, 2.
15. *Britannia and Trades' Advocate,* December 5, 1850, 2, *Hobart Town Courier,* December 7, 1850, 3.
16. *Hobart Town Courier*, December, 7,1850.
17. *Launceston Examiner,* December 4, 1850, 6.
18. http://seafarersmemorial.org.au/memorials/vessels/british_queen.php.
19. Tasmanian Parliamentary Paper (TPP) 74/1852:5.
20. Richard Davis and Stefan Petrow, *Varieties of Vice-regal Life*, 143; Tasmanian Parliamentary Paper no. 74/1852.
21. "New Dock and Constitution Dock", Tasmanian Parliamentary Paper no. 61/1852, 7.
22. Terry Newman, *Becoming Tasmania: renaming Van Diemen's Land* (Hobart: Parliament of Tasmania, 2005)
23. *Tasmanian Colonialist*, December 15, 1851, 2.
24. *Mercury*, January 13, 1858, 2.

25. *Cyclopedia of Tasmania,* I:197.
26. "Wharf and dock improvements" Tasmanian Parliamentary Paper no. 21/1855.
27. *Hobart Town Courier*, March 24, 1858, 2; *Tasmanian Telegraph*, October 30, 1858, 7.
28. Audrey Hudspeth and Linda Scripps, *Capital Port: a history of the Marine Board of Hobart* (Hobart: Hobart Ports Corporation, 2000): 43.
29. Des Wolfe, "Historical evolution old 23 Old Wharf", Department of Sea Fisheries, [Hobart] https://stors.tas.gov.au/au-7-0037-01023_1
30. *Cyclopedia of Tasmania,* 1901, I: 200.
31. *Mercury,* June 14, 1946, 4 , *Mercury*, February, 1950, 17.

Growing up at the Triabunna Barracks

Childhood at an east-coast property through the 19th and 20th centuries

AMELIA O'DONNELL

Children have been a part of Australia's human landscape since its beginnings.[1] And, from 1788, children of European descent began to leave their small footprints on this land.[2] The children of 19th and 20th century Tasmania were a constant presence in their communities, yet the lives of young people are significantly under-represented in narratives of Australia's past. Subsequently, it came as some surprise when children's artefacts were recovered during the archaeological investigations of the Tasmanian east coast property known as the Triabunna Barracks, a site whose 120-year-plus history is overshadowed by five years of British military occupation. The rediscovery of the child's presence at the Triabunna Barracks raised several questions, including who were they? And, what was life like for a child from a working-class family in Tasmania during the late 19th and early-20th centuries?

Employing the interdisciplinary tools of historical archaeology, a sub-discipline at the intersection of archaeology and history, I will present an in-depth interpretation of the child-related artefacts recovered from the Triabunna Barracks excavations which embody four themes visible in the assemblage — education, doll play, group games, and hand-made playthings. Through these analyses I will illustrate that although the lives of children at the barracks initially appear to reflect the ideals of childhood promoted

The Triabunna Barracks today.
Photo: Amelia O'Donnell

during the late 19th and early-20th centuries, if we dig a little deeper a more complex and nuanced narrative of childhood emerges.

■

Children of the past could make up to 40 per cent of their community, but their social and cultural impact has been neglected in academic research.iii This lack of attention stems from modern prejudices regarding what we think a child is and what childhood entails.[4] The modern-Western definition of a child is based on supposedly universal biological markers and we understand childhood to be a time when children do not actively contribute to the world.[5] Scholars have retroactively projected these views into the past, contending the child as an under-developed, passive member of a society was the same throughout all human history.[6] Archaeologists, too, have added to this prejudice, suggesting that past children left no identifiable physical traces.[7]

Only recently has the assumption of a historical continuity of the universal, passive child been recognised as incorrect. It is clear, even today, that the concept of childhood and the definition of children differs across cultures.[8] Currently, researchers recognise childhood to be a socio-cultural construct that can vary greatly, and children are now acknowledged as active cultural participants who do contribute to the material footprint of their society.[9] Historical archaeologists, too, have begun to break the bounds of scholarly prejudice to reveal the lived realities of children of the recent past.

Historical archaeologists study the remains of human activity from AD 1500 to the present.[10] In Australia, however, historical archaeology generally refers to the study of the post-European contact period, i.e., the beginnings of the Australia's written history. Historical archaeologists studying children of Australia's recent past can gain some understanding of the period-specific ideals of childhood and lives of children through historical sources such as household manuals, newspapers, and photographs.[11] However, historical sources were rarely created by children and the attitudes and ideals promoted in these works were constructed by influential, upper-class adults and were thus not attainable by all.[12] Therefore, interpreting the lives of Australian children through historical sources alone will not reveal the diversity of children's experiences.[13] However, the children obscured by written history still left behind physical traces.[14] Material culture, that is objects, embodies meaning and aspects of identity that are fundamental in socio-cultural constructs such as childhood meaning the artefacts left behind by the children of the Triabunna Barracks may hold valuable information regarding the realities of their childhood experiences.[15]

■

The Triabunna Barracks is a one-acre property located in the rural, coastal town of Triabunna, 84 kilometres north-east of Hobart, Tasmania. The property is listed on the Tasmanian Heritage Register as a "former barracks and stables" (Ref 1575) and two mid-19th century stone buildings and a functioning well survive on the property.[16] Historically, other two substantial buildings were present and a number of outbuildings would have also studded the site.[17]

The archaeological investigation of the Triabunna Barracks has occurred as part of the Triabunna Barracks Historic Archaeology Fieldschool.[18] The primary historical narrative connected to property is that it was a barracks constructed to house the British regiments charged with guarding the Maria Island convicts and the Tasmanian east coast from 1844 until 1850.[19] But this is period is only a small part of a long history.

The barracks property was purchased from the crown in 1844, and in late 1844 the land was sold to Joseph Hibbotson, who established The Freemasons' Arms Inn on the site.[20] In 1860 the inn was renamed The Spring Bay Tavern and the inn's name changed again around 1870 to The Retreat Inn.[21] The site functioned as a hotel until 1909.[22] In 1913 the Inn became the town's post office and functioned as the Triabunna bakery from 1930 until the late 1960s.[23]

After the bakery, the property was subject to demolition, re-development, and abandonment.[24] The Triabunna Barracks was a home for at least 20 families over its 125-year-plus history and the presence of children at the property would have been a common sight.[25] During their time at the barracks these children were cared for, they played, and contributed to their households, but their experiences are missing in the barracks' written history.[26] In spite of this, the barracks children are visible in the objects that were lost, hidden, discarded, and subsequently bought to light during the archaeological investigations of the Triabunna Barracks.

∎

As the investigations at the Triabunna Barracks are ongoing, the results presented here are based on representative but incomplete data. A broad range of artefacts, ranging in date from 1885 to the present, have been recovered from the barracks investigations, including ceramic tablewares, bottle glass, clay pipes fragments, butchered faunal remains, sewing items and building materials.[27]

Though the daily experiences of past Australians and their access to material culture could vary greatly, the artefact types recovered from the Triabunna Barracks mirror those found at other Australian historical sites indicating that the relatively rural Triabunna was strongly connected to a globalised network of material and idea exchange.[28] The barracks artefacts also suggest that, even though the occupants were working-class, they could participate in the performance of ideals, such as gentility, through the consumption of mass-manufactured materials.[29] It seems likely then that the lives of children at the barracks would have also been shaped by contextually specific and socio-culturally ascribed ideals of childhood.

∎

Child-related artefacts found at Triabunna Barracks include doll parts, marbles, plastic toys, writing implements and ceramics, and will represent less than 1 per cent of the total assemblage when investigations are complete (fig. 1). Children's artefacts have been recovered from the site's disturbed yard, and two rubbish dumps associated with the inn and bakery. The majority of the children's artefacts are relatively inexpensive types which date between the 1880s and 1930s, although some earlier and more modern objects are present (see fig. 1 N, O).[30] By the mid-1800s, childhood in the western world was considered a unique stage of the human lifecycle; it was a time of innocence and

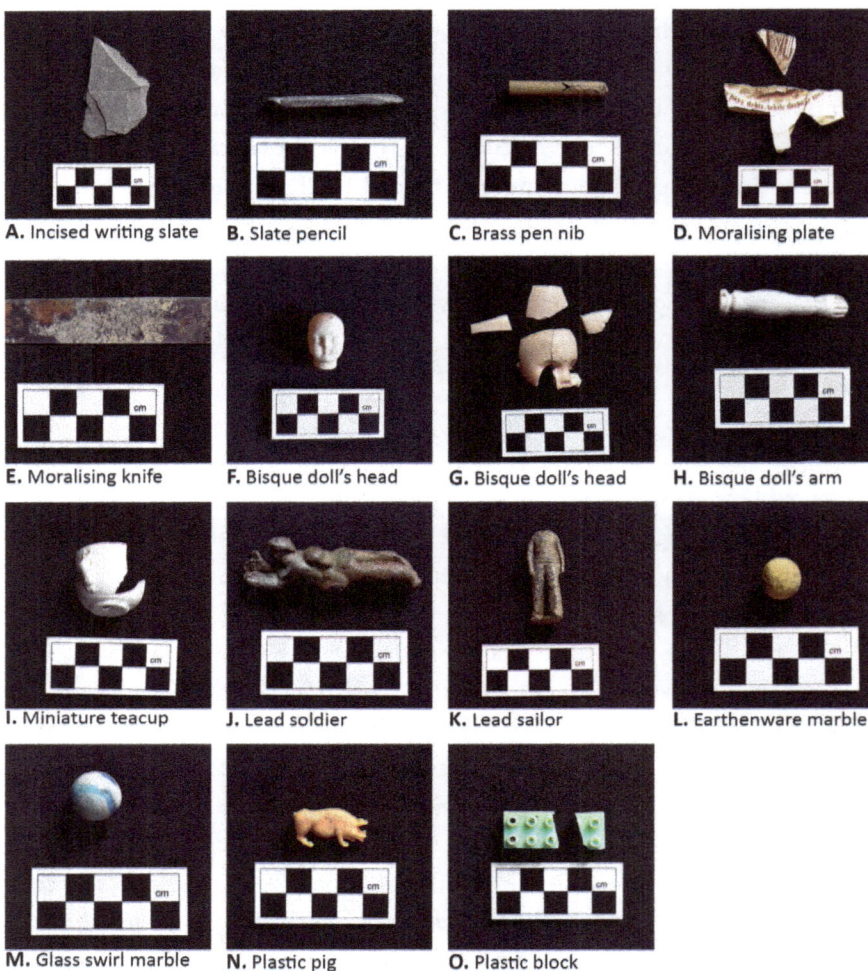

Figure 1: Children's objects found at the Triabunna Barracks.
Photo: Amelia O'Donnell

happiness, and play and toys had become the symbols of the child.[31] The presence of children's artefacts at the Triabunna Barracks suggests that, at least from The Retreat Inn phase, families were actively engaged with the evolving perceptions of childhood.[32] The occupants of the barracks did consider childhood to be a unique life stage and invested in the notion that children needed their own specific material culture, thus accepting that children were meant to play. Nevertheless, the realities of living in a rural area and at the location of the family's business may have hindered the adoption and implementation of all aspects of the ideal childhood package.³³ As such, I shall scrutinise the artefacts representing the themes of education, doll play, group games, and hand-made playthings to reveal the nuances of childhood at the Triabunna.

■

Education-focused artefacts comprise 38 per cent of the child-related artefacts recovered from the barracks and include objects relating to literacy and moral education. Artefacts relating literacy/numeracy education include slate fragments, slate pencils, graphite pencils, and pen nibs (see fig. 1 A–C). These writing implements were probably used by all members of a household, but the 1838 introduction of compulsory schooling in Tasmania and the presence of a school-house in Triabunna from 1863 mean these objects would have formed a significant portion of children's daily material interactions.³⁴ The implementation of compulsory schooling in the 19th century was a key turning point in construction of childhood as it separated children of all social classes from the concerns of the adult world.³⁵ The practice of literacy and numeracy was a part of the daily routine of the barracks children and nine of the 20 slate fragments recovered from the barracks are incised with lines indicating they were used for practising letters and possibly mathematics (see fig. 1 A).³⁶ Academic training at the barracks is supported by newspaper reports of the barracks children winning prizes at Triabunna school's annual awards day.³⁷ Along with their learning of letters and numbers, the barracks children also experienced moral education.

Two objects represent the moral education of the barracks children — fragments of a transfer-printed plate with the Benjamin Franklin maxim, "He that hath a trade hath an estate. At the working man's house hunger looks in but dare not enter ... for industry pays debts, while despair increaseth them", and a stainless-steel knife blade stamped with "FOR A GOOD CHILD" (see fig. 1 D, E).³⁸ The plate likely dates to the later decades of the 19th century and the knife post-dates 1913.³⁹ These moralising wares personify the idea that the moral education of children, needed to safeguard their innate goodness from the corruption of the outside world, was the duty of the household.⁴⁰ One of the primary training grounds of the home was the dining table, and although these artefacts promote different messages, the fact that both objects are made for dinning illustrates the parents of the barracks were forming and guiding their children's ethics through every day routines.⁴¹ Although there may have been some tension between the need for barracks children to contribute to the economy of the household and their schooling, it appears that the parents of the Triabunna Barracks embraced all opportunities to educate their children.[42] Education-focused artefacts primarily reveal the expectations of parents but these artefacts would have also been important for children's construction of their own sovereignty. They could claim ownership over them, incorporate them into their wider material suite, and choose whether or not they would absorb the lessons being imparted.[43] Writing materials and moralising wares were literal objects of education, but during the occupation of the barracks all children's artefacts, especially dolls, were considered to prepare children for their future.[44]

■

Evidence for doll play at the barracks comes in variety of forms including bisque doll parts, miniature teawares and lead military figures, making up 16 per cent of the children's materials (see fig. 1 F–K). Doll parts are one of the most enigmatic pieces of evidence for the child's presence at the barracks. Three to four heads, three limbs and a complete Kewpie doll have been recovered (see fig. 1 F–H).[45] In the 18th and early 20th century, dolls were promoted as feminine objects which indoctrinated girls into their appropriate gender roles through play.[46] The socialising function of dolls evolved over time but was always an aspirational influence for their young owners, encouraging them to be fashionable and socially literate ladies, and caring mothers competent in the skills of domesticity.[47]

The dolls and teawares at the Triabunna Barracks imply that young girls were participating in gender appropriate play. In contrast, the two post-World War I lead military figures, in the form of an American "doughboy" rifleman and sailor (see fig. 1 J–K), suggest the masculine ideals of militaristic-nationalism and violence were being encouraged in the play of the barracks boys.[48] Even though children often participated in doll play in socially ascribed ways, interpreting these artefacts based purely on gendered ideals is not realistic.[49] Of the 15 barracks families with children, all included children of both sexes and it seems unlikely that sharing would not occur between siblings. Furthermore, modern sociological studies have found that children in small, rural communities don't tend to divide themselves by gender when playing — they play with whomever they can — meaning the barracks children would have interacted with a range of toys and played in a range of ways not "appropriate" for their gender.[50] It must be remembered, however, that although adults may have purchased toys for children, play is generally controlled by children, and this is especially the case in group games.[51]

The presence of marbles is strong evidence for group play at the Triabunna Barracks. Ceramic and glass marbles of various sizes and patterns contribute 22 per cent of the children's assemblage (see fig. 1 L–M). Twenty of the 28 marbles recovered from the barracks are ceramic and the majority of these are inexpensive, earthenware types popular from the 1840s to the 1920s (see fig. 1 L).[52] The prevalence of earthenware marbles in the collection suggests these objects were either highly valued for their playing ability, or perceived specialness, or there was little concern surrounding their loss.[53] Importantly, the portability of these marbles demonstrates that even though there was a push to restrict children's movements outside the home from the middle of the 19th century, the children of the barracks did play beyond the protective gaze of adults and the domestic safe-haven of their home.[54] Although seemingly insignificant, marbles is a game of players and spectators and facilitates social interaction.[55] By playing a game of marbles, away from the expectations of adults, the children of the Triabunna Barracks would have cemented their place within a peer community through the creation, implementation and negotiation of rules and hierarchies.[56] Further, playing with others would allow these children to share, interpret, produce and reproduce socio-cultural knowledge.[57] The freedom and sociability of marble play would have also extended to play with other objects which may not have survived in the archaeological record of the barracks.

■

HAND-MADE PLAYTHINGS

The children's artefacts discussed so far have been mass-manufactured inorganic objects not subject to decay, but it is widely acknowledged that hand-made objects — often made from organic and natural materials — were the most common forms of playthings of past children.[58] Unfortunately, these play materials do not tend to survive in typical archaeological conditions, or are not recognised by archaeologists as playthings.[59]

Yet, the Triabunna Barracks did have one area where organic artefacts were preserved — the site's well. The waterlogged conditions of the well promoted an aerobic environment which hindered the decay of organic

Hand-made boat from the well on the Triabunna Barracks property.
Photo: Amelia O'Donnell

artefacts such as fabric, leather and wood. Only one child-related artefact was recovered from the well — the deck of a wooden miniature boat. The deck is from an object known as a pond yacht and the boat's nails broadly date the object to the 20th century.[60] The unique decoration and construction of the boat suggests it was one of the many hand-made objects that featured in the world of the barracks children. The finesse of the painted details, however, indicates the boat was more likely to be made by an adult than a child. The boat, therefore, represents some form of interpersonal negation between a child and adult, both of whom were actively engaging with the notion that children needed material culture for play — an ideal deeply ingrained into western culture by the 20th century.[61] A toy boat would have been seen as a natural plaything for a child of 20th century Triabunna and the creation of this boat likely reflects the importance of the sea in Triabunna's community identity, as well as the reproduction and reinforcement of this socio-cultural influence across generations.[62] By playing with this boat, the owner would have been constantly reinforcing and reinterpreting their identity as a child, and a member of the wider Triabunna community.

∎

CONCLUSION

The presence of children at the Triabunna Barracks should not have been unexpected, but their invisibility in the site's primary narrative and general written history meant that their experiences remained hidden until the materials they left behind were brought to light. The late 19th and early 20th century occupants of Triabunna Barracks were materially engaged with the socio-cultural ideals of their world, including the ideals of childhood. Even so, the artefacts recovered from the archaeological investigations at the barracks illustrate that there was some tension between the implementation of the idealised childhood and the lived experiences of these children. Though education-focused artefacts highlight the importance placed on the child as a scholar within the barracks families, they also represent an undercurrent of control on the part of the children.

Objects of doll play were also objects of tension between gender roles and the realities of play, while marbles — objects of group play — push the barracks children beyond the home, emphasising their active role in developing their own understanding of the world. The hand-made boat, on the other hand, represents children co-opting ideals from themselves and the value of play in connecting children with various aspects of their identity.

The children of the Triabunna Barracks were not passive receptacles of societal expectations. They were constantly and actively engaged in constructing their own lives and experiences within their family, their community, and the wider world. It is clear that children were at Triabunna Barracks and their experiences and histories should be acknowledged.

■ ■ ■

ENDNOTES

1. Jane Kociumbas, *Australian Childhood: A History* (St Leonards: Allen & Unwin Pty Ltd, 1997).
2. Jane Kociumbas, *The Oxford History of Australia. Volume 2, 1770–1860: Possessions* (Oxford: Oxford University Press, 1992), 6; Dianne Snowden, "'A Most Humane Regulation?': Free Children Transported with Convict Parents", *Papers and Proceedings: Tasmanian Historical Research Association* 58, No.1, (2011): 33–41.
3. Michelle C. Langley, "Magdalenian Children: Projectile Points, Portable Art and Playthings." *Oxford Journal of Archaeology* 37, No.1, (2018), 3.
4. Joanna Sofaer Derevenski, "Material Culture Shock: Confronting Expectations in the Material Culture of Children". In *Children and Material Culture*, ed. Joanna Sofaer Derevenski (London: Routledge, 2000), 5; Kathryn A. Kamp, "Where Have All the Children Gone?: The Archaeology of Childhood." Journal of Archaeological Method and Theory 8, No.1, (2001), 3.

5. Sofaer Derevenski, "Material Culture Shock", 5; Jane Eva Baxter, "The Archaeology of Childhood", *Annual Review of Anthropology* 37, (2008), 161.
6. Sofaer Derevenski, "Material Culture Shock", 7.
7. Baxter, "The Archaeology of Childhood", 162.
8. Helen B. Schwartzman, "Materializing Children: Challenges for the Archaeology of Childhood". In *Children in Action: Perspectives on the Archaeology of Childhood*, ed. Jane Eva Baxter, Archaeological Papers of the American Anthropological Association, 15 (Hanover: The Sheridan Press, 2005), 123–131.
9. Grete Lillehammer "The World of Children". In *Children and Material Culture*, ed. Joanna Sofaer Derevenski (London: Routledge, 2000), 20–22; Jane Eva Baxter, "Introduction: The Archaeology of Childhood in Context". In *Children in Action: Perspectives on the Archaeology of Childhood*, ed. Jane Eva Baxter, Archaeological Papers of the American Anthropological Association, 15 (Hanover: The Sheridan Press, 2005), 2; Kathryn A. Kamp, "Dominant Discourses; Lived Experiences: Studying the Archaeology of Children and Childhood". In *Children in Action: Perspectives on the Archaeology of Childhood*, ed. Jane Eva Baxter, Archaeological Papers of the American Anthropological Association, 15 (Hanover: The Sheridan Press, 2005), 115.
10. Dan Hicks and Mary C. Beaudry, "Introduction: The Place of Historical Archaeology". In *The Cambridge Companion to Historical Archaeology*, eds. Dan Hicks and Mary C. Beaudry (Cambridge: Cambridge University Press, 2006), 1.
11. Laurie Wilkie, "Not Merely Child's Play: Creating a Historical Archaeology of Children and Childhood". In *Children and Material Culture*, ed. Joanna Sofaer Derevenski (London: Routledge, 2000), 101.
12. Peter Davies and Adrienne Ellis, "The Archaeology of Childhood: Toys from Henry's Mill". *The Artefact* 28, (2005), 15; Susan Lampard "The Ideology of Domesticity and the Working-Class Women and Children of Port Adelaide, 1840–1890". *Historical Archaeology* 43, No.3, (2009), 50.
13. Harry Hendrick, *Children, Childhood and English Society, 1880–1990* (Cambridge: Cambridge University Press, 1997), 2–3.
14. Charles E. Orser Jr., *Historical Archaeology*, 3rd edn (New York: Routledge, 2017), 7.
15. Karin Calvert, *Children in the House: The Material Culture of Early Childhood, 1600–1900* (Boston: Northeastern University Press, 1992), 4; Sharon Brookshaw "The Material Culture of Children and Childhood: Understanding Childhood Objects in the Museum Context". *Journal of Material Culture* 14, No.3, (2009), 369.
16. D. A. Lenton, D. Wright, J. L. Flexner and C. J. Frieman, *Triabunna Barracks 3 Charles Street, Triabunna, Tasmania Research Plan & Archaeological Excavation Strategy* (Draft 4.0) (Canberra: Australian National University, Unpublished report 2015), 4.
17. "Friday November 12, The Retreat Inn, Spring Bay." *The Mercury*, November 1, 1886: 4, Retrieved from https://trove.nla.gov.au/newspaper/article/9128002; Brad Williams and Alan Townsend, *Statement of Historical Archaeological*

Potential: 3 Charles Street TRIABUNNA TASMANIA (Oatlands: Centre for Heritage at Oatlands, Unpublished report, 2015).
18. Lenton et al, *Research Plan & Archaeological Excavation Strategy*, 4.
19. Suzanne Lester, *Spring Bay Tasmania: A Social History* (Hobart: Artemis Publishing and Marketing Consultants, 1994), 29; Williams and Townsend, *Statement of Historical Archaeological Potential*, 10–12.
20. *The Hobart Town Gazette*, "Sale of Crown Lands". *The Hobart Town Courier and Van Diemen's Land Gazette*, May 3, 1844, 4. Retrieved from https://trove.nla.gov.au/newspaper/article/2951105; Maureen Martin Ferris, *3 Charles Street, Triabunna: History of The Military, Owners and Occupiers* (Unpublished report, 2016), 22.
21. "Spring Bay", *The Mercury*, December 8, 1862, 2. Retrieved from https://trove.nla.gov.au/newspaper/article/8813348; "Spring Bay", *The Mercury*, December 6, 1873, 2. Retrieved from https://trove.nla.gov.au/newspaper/article/8915291.
22. Martin Ferris, *Triabunna: History of The Military, Owners and Occupiers*, 26.
23. Ibid, 52–54.
24. Ibid, 52–58.
25. Ibid.
26. Colin Heywood, *A History of Childhood: Children and Childhood in the West from Medieval to Modern Times* (Cambridge: Polity Press, 2001), 37.
27. D. A. Lenton, J. L. Flexner, C. J. Frieman, P. T. Ricardi and D. Wright, *Triabunna Barracks 2016 3 Charles Street, Triabunna, Tasmania: Interim Report No.1 on Archaeological Fieldwork, Tasmanian Heritage Register (Ref 1575) (Final Draft 4.0)* (Canberra: Australian National University, Unpublished report 2016), 35.
28. Kociumbas, *Australian Childhood*; Susan Lawrence and Peter Davies, "Natives and Newcomers in the Antipodes: Historical Archaeology in Australia and New Zealand". In *International Handbook of Historical Archaeology*, eds. Teresita Majewski and David RM Gaimster (New York: Springer Science + Business Media, LLC, 2009), 629.
29. Lester, *Spring Bay Tasmania*; Penny Crook "Shopping and Historical Archaeology: Exploring the Contexts of Urban Consumption". *Australasian Historical Archaeology* 18, (2000), 17; Susan Lawrence "Exporting Culture: Archaeology and the Nineteenth-Century British Empire". *Historical Archaeology* 37, No. 1, (2003), 20–33; Lauren Prossor, Susan Lawrence, Alasdair Brooks and Jane Lennon, "Household Archaeology, Lifecycles and Status in a Nineteenth-Century Australian Coastal Community". *International Journal of Historical Archaeology* 16, No.4, (2012), 809–827.
30. Barbara A. Meissner, "Chapter 3: Dolls, Toys, Games, and Other Diversions". In *Archaeology at the Alamodome: Investigations of a San Antonio Neighbourhood in Transition, Volume III: Artifact and Special Studies*; Anne A. Fox, Marcie Renner and Robert J. Hard (San Antonio: Center for Archaeological Research, The University of Texas, Unpublished Report, 1997), 57–99; Peter Davies, *Henry's Mill: The Historical Archaeology of a Forest Community. Life around a Timber Mill in South-west Victoria, Australia, in the Early Twentieth Century* (Oxford: Archaeopress, 2006), 66–67; Margaretha Marie-Louise Vlahos, "Developing an

The University of Queensland, 2014) available from http://espace.library.uq.edu.au/view/UQ:344451.
31. Calvert, *Children in the House*, 80, 188–119; Kyle Sommerville, " 'A Place For Everything and Everything in its Place': The Cultural Context of Late Victorian Toys". In *The Archaeology of Childhood: Interdisciplinary Perspectives on an Archaeological Enigma*, ed. Güner Coşkunsu (Albany: State University of New York Press, 2015), 278.
32. Calvert, *Children in the House*; Hugh Cunningham, *Children and Childhood in Western Society Since 1500* (Harlow: Longman Group Limited, 1995), 41.
33. Jonathan Prangnell and Kate Quirk, "Children in Paradise: Growing up on the Australian Goldfields", *Historical Archaeology* 43, No.3 (2009), 38.
34. The Gazette, "Government Notices" *The Tasmanian*, December 14, 1838, 3, Retrieved from https://trove.nla.gov.au/newspaper/article/232803414; "Abstract of Government Advertisements" *The Mercury*, January 9, 1863, 2, Retrieved from https://trove.nla.gov.au/newspaper/article/8814291; Peter Davies "Writing Slates and Schooling." *Australasian Historical Archaeology* 23, (2005), 63.
35. David Nasaw, *Children of the City: At Work and at Play* (New York: Anchor Books, 1985), 41–48; Calvert, *Children in the House*, 60–61; Hendrick, *Children, Childhood and English Society*, 63–65.
36. Davies "Writing Slates and Schooling", 66.
37. For example "Spring Bay" The Mercury, December 31, 1881: 3, Retrieved from https://trove.nla.gov.au/newspaper/article/9004154.
38. Noel Riley, *Gifts for a Good Child: The History of Children's China 1790–1890* (Ilminster: Richard Dennis, 1991), 270–274.
39. Riley, *Gifts for a Good Child*, 13; Harold M. Cobb, *The History of Stainless Steel* (Materials Park; ASM International, 2010), 193.
40. *Australian Etiquette, or, the Rules and Usages of Best Society in the Australasian Colonies, Together with Their Sports, Pastimes, Games and Amusements*. Facsimile of original work published 1886 (Knoxfield: J. M. Dent 1980), 226–227; V. A. Crewe and D. M. Hadley " 'Uncle Tom Was There in Crockery': Material Culture and a Victorian Working-class Childhood." *Childhood in the Past* 6, No.2, (2013), 89–105.
41. Calvert, *Children in the House*, 127.
42. Hendrick, *Children, Childhood and English Society*, 63–65.
43. Crewe and Hadley, " 'Uncle Tom Was There in Crockery' ", 92.
44. Tania Andrade Lima, "The Dark Side of Toys in Nineteenth-Century Rio de Janeiro, Brazil", *Historical Archaeology* 46, No.3, (2012), 63–78.
45. Lila Rait, *Through the Nursery Window: A History of Antique Collectable Dolls in Australia, 1788-1950* (Melbourne: Oxford University Press Australia, 1989), 126-127.
46. Calvert, *Children in the House*, 110–111; Wilkie, "Not Merely Child's Play", 101.
47. Rait, *Through the Nursery Window*; Calvert, *Children in the House*, 117; Miriam Formanek-Brunell "Sugar and Spite: The Politics of Doll Play in Nineteenth Century America". In *Small Worlds: Children and Adolescents in America 1850-1950*, eds. Elliot West and Paula Petrik (Lawrence: University Press of Kansas, 1992), 107–124.

48. Donald C. Wellington and Joseph C. Gallo, "The March of the Toy Soldier: The Market for a Collectible", *Journal of Cultural Economics* 5, No.1, (1981), 69–70; Kociumbas, *Australian Childhood*, 146.
49. Calvert, *Children in the House*, 116–117; Formanek-Brunell, "Sugar and Spite", 121; Sommerville, "'A Place For Everything and Everything in its Place'", 290.
50. William A. Corsaro, *The Sociology of Childhood*, Fourth Edition. (Thousand Oaks: Sage Publications, Inc. 2015), 163, 168.
51. Wilkie, "Not Merely Child's Play", 100–113.
52. José E. Zapata, "Chapter 4: Alamodome and Abroad: A Composite Inquiry on Toy Marbles". In *Archaeology at the Alamodome: Investigations of a San Antonio Neighbourhood in Transition, Volume III: Artifact and Special Studies*; Anne A. Fox, Marcie Renner and Robert J. Hard (San Antonio: Center for Archaeological Research, The University of Texas, Unpublished Report, 1997), 108; Davies and Ellis, "Toys from Henry's Mill", 18.
53. Wilkie, "Not Merely Child's Play", 110; Margaretha Marie-Louise Vlahos, "Exploring the Experiences of Nineteenth-Century Colonial Children in Australia with the Application of Interpretive Reproduction Theory — An Alternative Approach in the Study of Childhood in the Past", *Childhood in the Past* 8, No.1, (2015), 56.
54. Nasaw, *Children of the City*; Hendrick, *Children, Childhood and English Society*; Wilkie, "Not Merely Child's Play", 110.
55. Wilkie, "Not Merely Child's Play", 110.
56. Corsaro, *The Sociology of Childhood*, 143, 221, 228; Vlahos, "Exploring the Experiences of Nineteenth-Century Colonial Children in Australia", 56.
57. Corsaro, *The Sociology of Childhood*, 127, 163.
58. Calvert, *Children in the House*, 113; Davies, *Henry's Mill*, 81–82; Eleanor Conlin Casella and Sarah K. Croucher, *The Alderley Sandhills Project: An Archaeology of Community Life in (Post)-Industrial England* (Manchester, Manchester University Press, 2010), 175–176.
59. Sally Crawford, "The Archaeology of Play Things: Theorising a Toy Stage in the 'Biography' of Objects", *Childhood in the Past* 2, No.1, (2009), 55–70; Jane Eva Baxter, "The Devil's Advocate or Our Worst Case Scenario: The Archaeology of Childhood Without Any Children". In *The Archaeology of Childhood: Interdisciplinary Perspectives on an Archaeological Enigma*, ed. Güner Coşkunsu (Albany: State University of New York Press, 2015), 19–36.
60. Tom Wells, "Nail Chronology: The Use of Technologically Derived Features", *Historical Archaeology* 32, No.2, (1998), 87.
61. Calvert, *Children in the House*; Corsaro, *The Sociology of Childhood*.
62. Alistair Roach, "Model Boats in the Context of Maritime History and Archaeology", *The International Journal of Nautical Archaeology* 37, No.2, (2008), 314.

ACKNOWLEDGMENTS

This research was supported by grant from the Carlyle Greenwell Research Fund. I would like to thank my supervisor Dr James Flexner for his encouragement and insights in my writing of this paper. I would also like to thank my co-supervisor Associate Professor Lesley Beaumont and the supervisors of the Triabunna Barracks Historic Archaeology Fieldschool for their support in my research endeavours. Finally, I would like to acknowledge the owners of the Triabunna Barracks, John and Kim Samin, without whom this research would not be possible.

The enigma of the Midlands arch

GINA SLEVEC

All that remains today of Horton College is the stoic yet commanding arch portico of the original building, which stands determined in a field amidst an expanding cherry crop by the Midlands Highway opposite Somercotes, just south of the township of Ross. This intriguing red brick and sandstone relic, familiar to so many north-south travellers, constitutes the residual structure of what was once a splendid educational institution that thrived in the second half of the 19th century in the historic and picturesque Midlands of Tasmania. Its story is a fascinating one that is emblematic of the richness of our remarkable island state's past.

■

In 1837, Captain Samuel Horton of Somercotes bequeathed 20 acres of land and £1,350 to the Wesleyan Methodist Church for the establishment of an elite boys' school. The foundation stone was laid on January 26, 1852, in the presence of about 200 people.[1] However, it was a further three years until the building was completed, due to the Victorian gold rush that drew labourers away from the area in pursuit of promised fortunes.

The College was not officially opened until October, 1855, with the first student, "John Manton aged 11 years admitted 3 October 1855".[2] He was one of 770 boys who passed through the college in its 37 years of operation, with an average of 50 students a year, mostly Tasmanian, although a number of pupils came from Victoria and New South Wales. Its most prosperous year was in 1872, when 86 boys were in attendance. The foundation stone for a new wing was laid on December 8, 1862, and was completed near the close of the following year. It is interesting to note Keith Sykes' editorial comment on this in his transcription of the *Journal of Horton College*, whereby he wondered, "Where they put the 64 in the little room afforded by the original building is a mystery ... it must have been a close pack."[3]

Based on the tradition of the English public schools of the era, Horton was promoted as a healthy educational environment in which future colonial trailblazers could gain a superior education in the heart of the Tasmanian countryside. Subject offerings included Latin, Greek, French, algebra, trigonometry, history, Geography, arithmetic, writing, grammar and scripture, along with music, drawing and drill. A flier for the college advertised education and board at £50 per annum (£60 for students aged above 15), with additional costs for washing, medical attendance, music, drawing and drill. At the time, and in the modern equivalent, this was a substantial fee that could only be afforded by the wealthiest of families. Indeed, many eminent Tasmanian families sent their boys to be educated at Horton College, the register including familiar names such as Kermode, Riggall, Pitt, Archer, Davies, Solomon, Burgess, Crooke and Allport, among many others.

■

The Masters of Horton came from far and wide, but their qualifications were not always above board. In the unique Tasmanian style, things did not always go according the strictest of plans at Horton College, and the result is a story that is both intriguing and complex. The *Horton College Journal* reveals — amidst a prevalence of details of day-to-day life — that there were indeed scandalous appointments exposing academic imposters, and dramatic events that transpired in the remote midlands setting.

An entry dated September 23, 1859, states, "Mr Maxey, the Head Master, left to the great satisfaction of the President and Masters who had all been insulted by him."[4] This reflects a difficulty the college administration faced, with staff who often proved difficult and unreliable. In the previous year, documented on December 21, "Thomas Melville [was] dismissed from his situation in deep disgrace and heavily in debt. A desperately bad man."[5] There were also issues with teachers presenting with falsified qualifications: on June 6, 1856, "B. Atkinson dismissed for incompetency. A regular impostor."[6]

In addition to the problems the masters at times presented, other troubles plagued the College. In 1876 *The Mercury* in Hobart featured a report of a case heard at the Police Court by the magistrate in Ross on Monday, September 4, instigated by the aforementioned Mr Edwin Maxey. The headmaster, William Fox, was accused of severely beating a student, Edwin Maxey, son of the former headmaster, and allegedly contributed to his "nervous derangement".[7] It seems that the young boy had a history of misbehaving and causing trouble (like his father, it would seem) having been punished for disrespect during prayers, leaving the college without permission, writing a "naughty, witty letter"[8] and the like. While his punishments of being hit about the head with the headmaster's hand and slipper may seem harsh, they were not unusual or excessive for the time, as the magistrate decided.

Following this, the newspaper published a series of letters to the editor regarding "Discipline at Horton College". Letters were penned by his parents, Edwin and Jane Maxey, along with William Fox and Reverend George B. Richards, the President of the College. There are many highly charged lines in the letters, whereby Fox defended his behaviour against what he claimed was "so ridiculous a charge".[9] while the Maxeys railed on with accusations of how the boy was "shamefully and unjustly punished, being accused of faults he never committed".[10] What they ultimately reveal is a rather sordid episode in which headmaster Fox emerged victorious against the aggrieved Maxeys, to the reported cheers of his pupils who attended the trial.

Journal entries in later years of the college's operation had become more sparing, and no reference was made to this case. Nevertheless, these articles provide readers with the particulars of a story that was undoubtedly quite a scandal, whilst also revealing the rich tapestry of the characters and culture of the period and place.

■

A typical day for the boys of Horton began with the school bell calling them to rise at 6.30 a.m., when they would be taken out on the road for drill, followed by their lessons which concluded at 4pm. Dinner was at 5.30 p.m. and bedtime was strictly 8.30 p.m. Sundays offered the boys an extra half hour in bed before prayers and breakfast, followed by the boys walking two to three abreast the two and a half miles into Ross for the weekly church service. On return, after lunch at 1pm, they were free to enjoy the outdoors or write letters home.

There were half-yearly examinations in mid-June, and end of year public examinations in December. Annual prize ceremonies were held on the conclusion of these, awarding prizes for excellence in the array of subjects and classes, along with awards for writing proficiency and improvement,

Horton College, Ross, Tasmania.
Tasmanian Archive and Heritage Office

reading and recitation. The annual Horton Scholarship was awarded, worth £20, donated by Mrs Horton of Somercotes. There were also awards for other aspects of academic endeavour and behaviour, including good conduct and diligence.

In 1863 the masters adopted a plan of awarding 18 marks per week to each of the boys. Marks were forfeited for transgressions of the school rules, and each Saturday the marks were read out. "All those who have the 18 are put down on the Boni list, and are entitled to go out in the bush the ensuing week."[11]

Academic endeavour was taken seriously at Horton College, as the primary means of business. This was evident in the rigour of lessons and the celebrations of achievements in annual prize-giving ceremonies. Outstanding positions in the "examination for exhibition" could even mean a day off for all the pupils: "Cecil Allport won an Exhibition. He stood second. A Holiday."[12]

■

Like any good boarding school history, there is an array of documented tales of lads being lads, enjoying the usual boyish activities along with some mischief and adventures beyond the confines of the classrooms. The promised healthy rural situation of the school did indeed provide opportunities for wider learning and a chance to grow beyond the lessons and textbooks. Most were quite harmless, but this was not always the case.

Free hours spent roaming the countryside, involvement with sports including cricket and athletics, and springtime bird egg collecting suggest a life of the boys that enhanced and balanced that of their formal education. A popular pastime in free hours was trips up to one of the "cabooses — small huts made of stones with roofs thatched with grass — and to spend the day after the style of Stalky and Co.",[13] enjoying outdoor meals of chipped potatoes, boiled rabbits and damper. Being outside also gave the boys a chance to "indulge in surreptitious smokes",[14] and it was not uncommon for a clay pipe and some fig tobacco to be produced by the students and used to tempt other boys.

In 1872 a "very large iron gymnasium and play shed"[15] was constructed, which one would imagine to be highly popular, particularly on inclement days. There were special occasions marking important dates such as the president and queen's birthdays, featuring great bonfires and fireworks to celebrate. There must have been much for the boys to write about in their letters home to their families.

There were stories of incidents such as the bushrangers' attack at Somercotes that established themselves as legends for the boys:

> It seems that during 1843 Martin Cash, the noted bushranger, afterwards pardoned, made a visit to "Somercotes", took the inmates completely by surprise and finally bailed up the Captain when he rushed to see what was causing a commotion in the place ... the Captain, standing with his back to the fireplace, was saying "You may shoot me Cash, but God will protect me. I am not afraid to die, but you are." Bullet marks on the doorway of one of the rooms at "Somercotes" ... were always an object of awed interest to the boys of the College who were fortunate enough to go and see them.[16]

No doubt such stories fuelled the boys' imaginations and emotions; their games of bushrangers launching surprise attacks on innocent travellers, acted out in the bushland around the school can be easily imagined.

The boys were also known to be up for a bit of mischief. An anecdote published in *The Mercury* by a Horton old boy tells the tale of "a runaway marriage of two town and country families" at a time when "the high spirited boys of a family were often sent to Horton College in order to try the disciplinary effect

Masters and Pupils of Horton College.
Tasmanian Archive and Heritage Office

of country air".[17] In this instance, the boys were called upon to cut the telegraph lines between Hobart and Launceston so that the enamoured pair might escape in their pursuit of love without intervention. The boys readily obliged: "They would, and they did."[18]

There are myriad references to the boys' indulgences in contraband substances such as tobacco, midnight feasts and pillow fights, boyish escapades (and no doubt scraps) and sneaky sips of "a sort of raspberry squash"[19] from concealed bottles in Sunday church. The local baker, nicknamed Doughy by the boys, came twice a week to deliver bread and a great treat was the arrival of the "tuck shop", a "chaise cart loaded with 6d packets of sweets"[20] that was clamoured about as soon as the horse has come to a standstill.

■

On warm afternoons the boys were sometimes released from class an hour early and went off down the track to enjoy some hours of bathing in the Macquarie River. It was a popular pastime, along with boating and fishing, but there were dangers at times. The *Journal of Horton College* documents such an event on February 14, 1890, when "a flood came suddenly down the Macquarie River while the boys were bathing. They just had time to get out of the water and save their clothes."[21] There were several records about the flooding river that, at times, prevented pupils from Ross making it to school, along with scheduled trips for sporting events. In 1863 there were "calamitous floods" which, upon subsiding, saw, "Extensive and deep chasms in the road. Indeed the waters had been breaking like billows over it near the bridge. An attempt to cross was fatal to Mr McCraken of Launceston, and others, madly attempting, narrowly escaped."[22]

One can only imagine the chaos and danger of such a dramatic event in the remote Midlands of Tasmania in the middle of the 19th century.

There were also dramas and even tragedies that befell the Horton boys in its years of operation, including unofficial departures — on June 16, 1857, "James J. Turnbull ran away from College,"[23] which prompted questions as to why and where.

The school journal documents two deaths in the school: "Two of the boarders, Frederick Walter Dally and George English Herbert Fulton died. In the former case death was caused by accident, and in the latter it was the result of disease to which the boy had shown a predisposition before he entered the school."[24]

Mr R. T. White's letter to *The Mercury* in response to an article on the College, mentions a "sad and mysterious"[25] incident, "A servant, going out into the yard to ring the getting-up bell was horror-struck to see the lifeless body of a boy suspended from a dormitory window, a tragic ending to some boyish escapade."[26]

One might presume this to be the same poor boy.

■

With diminishing enrolments, "caused by a deep economic depression",[27] and the establishment of private schools in Hobart and Launceston, Horton College's prosperity began to decline in the late 1880s.

Following the arrival of The Reverend J. de Q. Robin in April 1889, who commenced his duties as headmaster the following month,[28] female students began to be mentioned in the school *Journal*. Miss Marion Riggall and Miss Jane Riggall were noted in the prize distribution lists in the years from 1884 to 1890, and "Miss G[ertrude] de Q. Robin proved to be the dux of the school for 1892 and would have gained the Horton Scholarship if it had been awarded."[29] There were also female teachers employed, with a reference to "Miss Taylor's pupils"[30] in the music prizes in 1883.

A Mr Steer took over the college for a short period of time after the official closure of Horton, commencing in 1893, with the intent of maintaining a private boarding college, but his "claimed qualifications were bogus. He did not have a BA from Dublin. The College Council found out his deception."[31] Mr Steer ran the school into further debt, "so that everything [of] worth had to be sold off leaving a debt of £160 or more."[32] It was a sad end for Horton College. Within barely a year of Mr Steer's occupancy, it was closed as a school for the final time in 1894.

In his transcription of the *Journal* of Horton College, editor Keith Sykes notes the,

> ... somewhat sad irony that the College was cursed at both the beginning and end of its existence by staff members who were imposters. Nevertheless, the careful oversight that the Church exercised through the Presidents was able to build a school whose influence for good on the lives of hundreds of boys and young men can never be measured.[33]

Despite the challenges and dramas, the tragedies and transgressions, this reflection of Mr Sykes' encapsulates what was the ultimate accomplishment and legacy of Horton College — a truly great educational institution that is such a strong thread in the tapestry of our Tasmanian past and our identity.

There was a stipulation that should the establishment cease to operate as a school, the property would revert to the control of the Somercotes family. With the departure of Mr Steer, and the later vacation of the building by the Riggalls, this eventuality proved to be the case. As such, the end of a remarkable era was reached.

In 1917 the building was sadly torn down — it was speculated this was due to a shortage of resources in the World War I. There were also rumour of a fire, although there is no evident record to substantiate this. Some of the bricks were used to build a cottage on the site, while others were recycled.

The legacy of Horton College remains in the continued presence of the arch as a fascinating reminder of its existence, and features of the building that were preserved and recycled. The original bell from Horton College was relocated to Hutchins School in Hobart, while a number of bricks from the building were used to construct a wall of the Mary Fox Wing of the Methodist Ladies College, now Scotch Oakburn College, in Elphin Road, Launceston.

All that remains: the portico arch.
Photo: Gina Slevec

The "Methodist Ladies College, opened in 1886, aimed at providing girls with the same educational advantages offered boys at Horton College, Ross." [34] Mary Elizabeth Gertrude Fox, the "daughter of William Fox, Headmaster of Horton College, 1863–89," [35] was educated there before completing a BA at the University of Tasmania, and was "appointed Headmistress of the Methodist Ladies College in 1903, aged 26." [36]

Today, the site of the school remains largely untouched, with scattered relics hidden amongst the weeds that protect and conceal the mysteries and tales of the past. Beyond the stoic brick and sandstone remains, the stories of those who attended the school and the historical records leave Tasmanians with a captivating and rather comprehensive record of an eminent and intriguing school, the legacy of which remains even if its walls do not. May the enigma of Horton College, such a fascinating and remarkable feature of Tasmania's colonial history, endure in our collective imagination.

■ ■ ■

ENDNOTES

1. E. R. Pretyman, 2018. "Some Notes On Horton College, Once, A Well-Known School Near Ross, Tasmania". *Eprints.Utas.Edu.Au*. https://eprints.utas.edu.au/14372/1/1958_Pretyman_Horton_College.pdf.
2. Keith Sykes, (Ed) *Journal of Horton College, Ross* (2005).
3. Sykes, *Journal*.
4. Sykes, *Journal*.
5. Sykes, *Journal*.
6. Sykes, *Journal*.
7. "Discipline at Horton College", "To the Editor of *The Mercury*", *The Mercury* (Hobart, Tas.: 1860–1954), September 9, 1876. *Trove*. https://trove.nla.gov.au/newspaper/article/8947801?searchTerm=discipline%20at%20horton%20college%20%20%20%20%20%20%20%20%20%20%20&.
8. "Discipline", September 9, 1876.
9. "Discipline at Horton College", "To the Editor of *The Mercury*", *The Mercury* (Hobart, Tas.: 1860–1954), September 11, 1876. *Trove*. https://trove.nla.gov.au/newspaper/article/8947821?searchTerm=discipline%20at%20horton%20college%20%20%20%20%20%20%20%20%20%20%20&.
10. "Discipline at Horton College", "To the Editor of *The Mercury*", *The Mercury* (Hobart, Tas.: 1860–1954), September 18, 1876". *Trove*. https://trove.nla.gov.au/newspaper/article/8947961?searchTerm=discipline%20at%20horton%20college%20%20%20%20%20%20%20%20%20%20%20.
11. "Horton College, Ross", *The Mercury* (Hobart, Tas.: 1860–1954), December 23, 1863". *Trove*. https://trove.nla.gov.au/newspaper/article/8823411.
12. Sykes, *Journal*.
13. "Horton College — Its Founding and History A Famous Australian School", *The Mercury* (Hobart, Tas.: 1860–1954), December 27, 1920. Trove. https://trove.nla.gov.au/newspaper/article/11507689.
14. "Horton College — Its Founding and History".
15. "Horton College — Its Founding and History".
16. Pretyman, "Some Notes".

17. R. T. White, "Horton College — From an Old Boy", *The Mercury* (Hobart, Tas.: 1860–1954), January 9, 1930. *Trove*. https://trove.nla.gov.au/newspaper/article/29149299?searchTerm=horton%20college%20%20%20%20%20.
18. White, "Horton College".
19. "Horton College — Its Founding and History".
20. "Horton College — Its Founding and History".
21. Sykes, *Journal*.
22. Sykes, *Journal*.
23. Sykes, *Journal*.
24. Sykes, *Journal*.
25. White, "Horton College".
26. White, "Horton College".
27. Sykes, *Journal*.
28. Sykes, *Journal*.
29. Sykes, *Journal*.
30. Sykes, *Journal*.
31. Sykes, *Journal*.
32. Sykes, *Journal*.
33. Sykes, *Journal*.
34. Jo Oliver, and David Morris. 2018. "Scotch Oakburn College". *Utas.Edu.Au*. http://www.utas.edu.au/library/companion_to_tasmanian_history/S/Scotch%20Oakburn.htm.
35. Jo Oliver, 2018. "Mary Fox". *Utas.Edu.Au*. http://www.utas.edu.au/library/companion_to_tasmanian_history/F/Mary%20Fox.htm.
36. Oliver, "Mary Fox".

Job in Tasmania

KEES WIERENGA

Gerald's face lit up when I showed him the program. Sixty-three years disappeared, and as he turned the pages he began to sing all the songs. "That was the party," he said, "that finished at five o'clock in the morning."[1]

It was a party that once seemed a normal expectation and then seemed impossible. Twenty-five years earlier there was a vague knowledge that, all things being equal, this party would eventually happen. Life would be mostly good, the marriage would probably be blessed with children, and everyone would live happily ever after.

The children did come, closely followed by very dark days. At first, the presence and behaviour of the Nazi invader was quite benign, but they slowly became nasty. Impositions were made, each new demand harsher than the last. Food and consumables were rationed. Jews were forced at gunpoint to migrate to the east. Ex-soldiers were commanded to return to duty, possibly to be cannon fodder on the eastern front. Young men were dragooned into work groups to labour in the factories of the Nazi war machine.[2]

Many people resisted the decrees by disappearing, although sometimes only for a short period. Pieter Laning hid on a small island in the wetlands near his city. He complained of being sodden several times from torrential downpours, and of being bored witless. In later years he would regard it as a garden of Eden, but after the season of *razzias* in Groningen ended, he was happy to return home.[3]

The thousands of people who disappeared underground, literally and figuratively, all needed food which could only be obtained with appropriate documentation. People sympathetic to the plight of those underground, and actively involved in helping them survive, formed a loose association of resisters to the regime. The regime labelled them "terrorists" and hunted for them. Resistance workers who had been caught were violently interrogated and deprived of food, comfort and medical assistance, if they were lucky.[4]

After the war, a small group of Resistance workers, men who had entrusted their lives to each other, resolved to begin a new life as far as they could from the terror, horror and blunder they had endured. They settled in Kingston, Tasmania, in 1950,[5] and four years later, they celebrated. The celebration was bigger than anything they had had so far — far bigger than the wedding of Wim to a glove representing his bride (in Holland) so that she would be protected by a wedding ring when she travelled to join him.[6] It was also bigger than the wedding of two Dutch migrants in 1952. The Warden of Kingborough at that time was pleased to have this event recorded in the council minutes, along with his hope that there would be many more.[7] Many Kingston people were involved in that celebration, including the school master and the grocer, who thrived on the memory to the end of her days.[8]

But this wedding anniversary celebration was much bigger than anything before, because it was a celebration of life. Pieter Laning took on the organisation of the event. He was the most lively, inventive and energetic member, and also the prankster, in his cohort.[9] Two years earlier he had complained of pain in his back every time he coughed. The diagnosis of TB forced almost a year's medical treatment and bed rest, just when he was getting into his stride in his new country.[10] He remembered the extreme pain he had endured in the horror of the Bay of Lubeck bombing, where so many suffered all the torments of hell, a place beyond the screams of agony, where thousands abandoned all hope of living. Then he had been in the wrong place, with the end of life in sight. Now he was in the right place, as Tasmania led the Commonwealth in the control and treatment of TB, and an end to the illness was in sight.[11]

Pieter sent out invitations to the migrant community, and called for entertainment submissions.[12] Choirs were formed and skits prepared, stage names were invented or imposed, songs were composed and rehearsed, a program was devised and typed and printed. Gaps on the page were filled with line drawings by Pieter, or with the favourite proverbs of the guests, or advertisements — all invented by the self-appointed Master of Ceremonies. He might have been laid low by illness but now he was on top of the world.

A photo of the happy couple, looking plump and content, standing in front of their new home, was fixed to every copy of the program to celebrate the

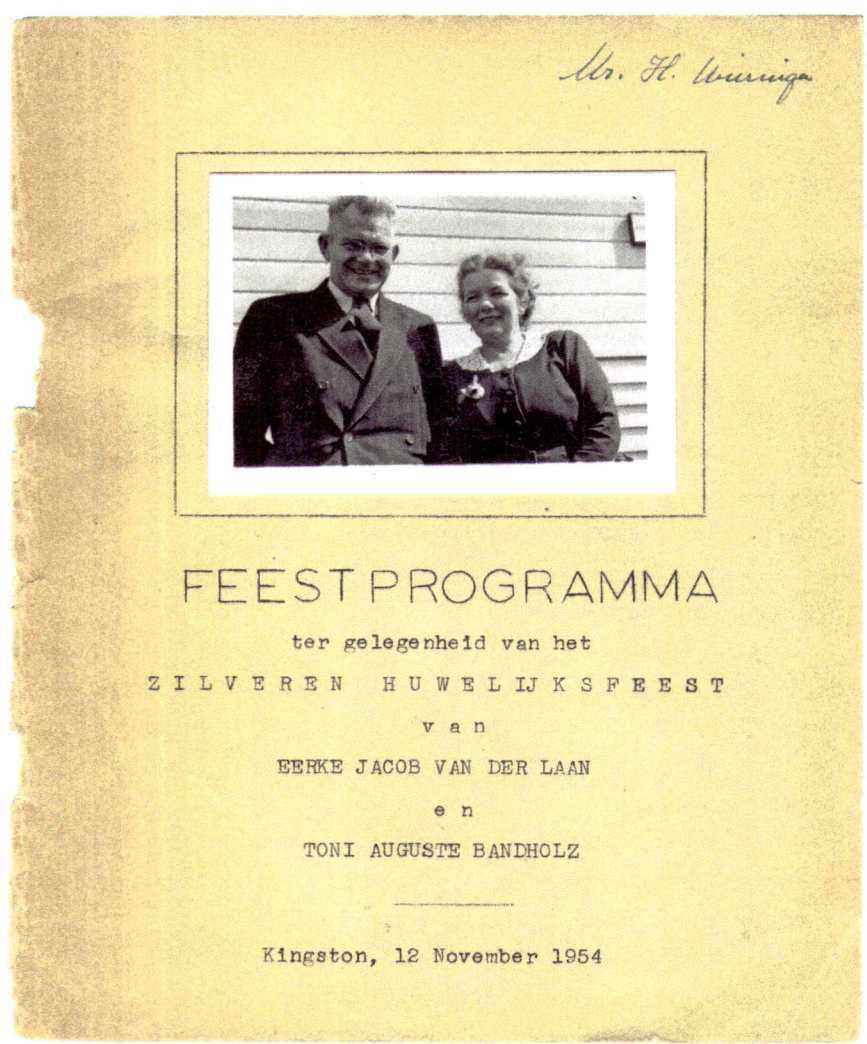

Cover of the program for the twenty-fifth wedding anniversary celebration.
Wierenga family collection

twenty-fifth wedding anniversary of Eerke van der Laan and Toni Bandholz, at Kingston, November 12, 1954. The American Gothic pose has been arranged by the photographer to minimise the difference in height of a couple sometimes called one and a half cents.[13]

Before the war, Eerke had been a champion gymnast, invited to compete in the 1924 Olympic Games (which he declined because he refused to compete on Sundays).[14] Towards the end of the war, he survived a forced march from the concentration camp to Lubeck Bay, where the witnesses of the Nazi atrocities were loaded on ships to be scuttled in the Baltic Sea. A blunder by the RAAF destroyed the ships in the harbour, and few survived.[15] When Eerke finally dragged the forty-five remaining kilograms of his six-foot frame back home, his family thought a bundle of rags had been abandoned on their doorstep.[16]

Eerke used his administration skills to achieve a lot. In Tasmania, he was equally happy to have builders' tools in his hands, or to prepare a church service. Fluent in English and German since school,[17] he was always ready to use his skills or to put his hand to whatever else was needed to help others. He was regarded as a leader by all, noted, inter alia, by *The Mercury*,[18] but he preferred the privilege of service. Toni filled the role of rock, solid as the dolerite of a Tasmanian mountain, in their busy life.

At 8 p.m., in Number Two workshop of the Australian Building Corporation (ABC) in Little Groningen, Kingston, the celebration began with a word and a prayer from their pastor, Rev Y van der Woude. This was immediately followed by all singing Psalm 103:1: "Now thank we all our God". This was sung in Dutch, and the whole program was conducted in Dutch, despite rule 10 in the program insisting that it was compulsory for everybody to speak English that evening.

Only one verse of one song in the program was composed in English, and printed with the notation "sing cheerfully and happy". Somehow it was expected that the only local girl in their midst would be willing to sing about the Dutch boy she fancied, with words written by a person she vaguely knew, in front of hundreds of Dutchies. Kingston people loved the Dutch migrants in their community and had established many strong personal links.[19] The Kingborough Council preferred them above British migrants,[20] and there was a shared vision for a more prosperous future together, but April was neither cheerful nor happy, just a super embarrassed teenager, and hid under the table when her turn came to declare her love in song.[21]

Rule 17 in the program stipulated that the utmost respect needed to be shown to the Jenever Functionaries — an invented title for the persons in charge of dispensing alcoholic drinks. Their task, anticipating RSA courses and certificates by forty years, was bolstered by the many invented proverbs in the program that encouraged drinking in moderation. They could not know that their role would eventually be one shot of a broadside that could be fired against the doctoral assertion by Julian [22] that the group was teetotal. Smoking, on the other hand, was only frowned upon by evangelical and fundamentalist Christians.[23] Cigarettes were placed in tumblers for guests to enjoy liberally, and the aroma of cigars was enjoyed by all.

∎

One of the songs composed for the celebration related the highlights of the Dover High School job, set to a familiar Dutch tune about windmills. Another, written to fit a Saint Nicholas tune, ran to thirteen verses, each a little story about events in the life of the individual nominated to sing it. Some details were quite personal, speaking of far away love.

Item six on the program gave the opportunity for speeches to be made in response to the two official speeches. It was noted that, should inspiration be lacking at this point, opportunity would be given after drinks. After several songs sung communally, Bart gave a graphic presentation. The painter in the Company, he had had time to hear and reflect as he wielded his brush. He had collected intelligence for the Allies during the war, so a light-hearted report on the gossip of the ABC was easy to do. He had been number one on the list of terrorists wanted by the Gestapo in Gronigen,[24] and was convinced that the Lord gave him the right words to say on the several occasions when they could have taken him. Now he carried a legacy of painful memories, as well as some hearing loss and nagging headaches, which he accepted just as the Apostle Paul accepted his torment.[25] Otherwise he went on to live a long, full life, right up to the end.[26]

Bart's piece was followed by a presentation of "The Model Commander" (loosely based on a Gilbert & Sullivan work), made in Dutch by three of the women. They also presented a skit about newborns which probably resonated well amongst the audience of mostly young families. The average age of the group was 37, because many were late starters. The war had put so many lives on hold, that three babies in five years was the new norm.[27]

Food was rarely mentioned in writings of the period, except when novel or exceptional. In the winter of 1950, Eerke and his best friend Ep had been nominated to be the "Joshua and Caleb" of the ABC group. They had first scouted northern Tasmania, and experienced a meat pie in Launceston — which they described as a pastry with a hot, but undefinable, filling. Nothing else appealed to them either, and they were advised to seek their future south of Hobart.[28]

Blissfully unaware that there were only two buses from Hobart to Kingston each day, they missed the nine-thirty and started walking. Archie Smith came by, gave them a lift, gave them work, gave them connections to government, and gave them lunch — barbecued lamb chops that he especially went to the butcher for, and a can of green peas, cooked on a campfire on the building block. They described this meal as a banquet fit for a king, with power to transport their minds to beautiful places.[29]

The Australian "bring a plate" concept which allowed an open invitation to an event and guaranteed there would be sufficient food was novel. Yet at this celebration the equivalent of "grub's up" was used to describe supper, without further description or comment.

After supper, there were many other skits and presentations of which we know the name or the presenter, but nothing else. In some instances even that cannot be known because nicknames are used, such as Sik, Wik and Dik, or "The Dutch Flowers of Kingston". In all, there were 14 presentations before the main event, a performance by a choir, formed for the occasion, that called itself the Bird Song Singers.

The choir was introduced with bombast and fiction. The audience were told that the celebration committee had made a huge effort to obtain the services of the world famous conductor of the "Bird Song Singers of Kingston", Mr Cornelianos du Overeemos (in penguin suit with flapping wings), and he was prepared to give a performance tonight with his famous youth choir. They had just this last week finished a jubilant tour through Europe and the Scandinavian islands, it was said.

The choir was scheduled to perform eleven items, all with some attention to quality music and an emphasis on generating laughs. The members of the choir were all given fantastic, nonsense names and impossible, nonsense talents. Nonsense was allowed to happen because that was part of enjoying life, of experiencing the gaps in the rules of life, of indulging in the complexity and joy of being. It was an expression of the joy of the liberation, of having the world at your feet, of the freedom available to the children of God, children who enjoyed their relationship with their Father, the Creator of everything including playing with nonsense.

The choir members included Little Luutje, who was quite a big man and would probably have earned the same moniker in the Australian vernacular. Geertje Mus was described as a hoarse tenor, but the reason for the description is lost in the mists of time. Young Schut, with his ever-cheeky grin, sang heavy bass although he was a small man. Storming Joopie had storm in his name, so his moniker was a lazy play with words, and he sang alto. His wife was a well-known musician and choir master. Little Wigger was the only son of the celebrating couple, twenty years old and by far the youngest in the group. The moniker was a little dig at his youth, a hint that his voice had not yet broken, so he must be a rising tenor. Tommy Moustache was described as a soprano bass. His Resistance name had been Tom, and it had stuck. Once a registrar, he had destroyed many civil records so that people ceased to exist to the Gestapo, besides stealing ration coupons.[30] He was always convinced that he was marked for assassination for his war work, and therefore carried a pistol in the small of his back until his dying day.[31]

Little Rieks was six feet tall and as strong as an ox, one of the men who had one plate of potatoes and a separate plate of vegetables with a small piece of meat, maybe a meatball, for dinner. Every harvest five one-hundredweight sacks of potatoes were tipped into a purpose-built holding bin in his pantry, to keep him fuelled through the winter. He was listed as the whistler, and performed a solo. Driessy Murk was a challenge for the program maker — Pieter couldn't find a stage name for this man, who also sang soprano. Wimmy Sik was probably the sort of man who would sing if he thought he was alone — he was descibed as an open window singer. Jackie from the Dam was actually Jack and didn't come from anywhere near a dam, but the word was in his name. He sang sometimes alto, sometimes bass. Picky Kroon completed the group and sang mezzo soprano. He had a bass voice and a well-earned reputation as a fastidious joiner.

■

The program also included items that involved audience participation and recitations, jokes and the like, performed by the gentlemen Steen, de Haan, Pinkster, van Betlehem, van Herweijnen, Mosterd and de Vries. The gentlemen Slot and Balkema were insufficiently organised to have their song printed, but they had promised, according to the program, to sing a duet.

At five o'clock on Sunday morning, Murk's Janny (there were several Janny's) led the party in a closing song. The words are on page 33 of the program:

> Goodnight, we're going to bed
> The day has been good

> We celebrated with each other
> The silver wedding feast
> Together we close this day
> 'T was a celebration that is seldom seen
> So happy and free, so happy and free.

The translation is clumsy, but the lines rhyme in the Dutch original. The words speak of being happy (*blij*) because they need to rhyme with free (*vrij*), but their lives were actually filled with joy. As the ABC they had been able to build new homes for themselves, with front doors that were never locked. As butcher, baker and candlestick maker, they had acquired building skills and built houses and schools for the people of Tasmania. They would go on to build the new era — service stations, public pools, and TV studios.[32]

The memory of being unhappy and of lacking freedom, of a time when their lives had been put on hold by the war, deprived of opportunity and growth, was not yet faded. They had put their lives in danger for the sake of strangers in response to the call of the Gospel. Some had suffered brutal treatment, deprived of food, warmth and medicine. Families had lived in fear of betrayal and discovery in a world where no one could be trusted. Families had worried due to lack of news about fathers and brothers sucked into the violent world of the Gestapo, of their brutal prisons, torture chambers and concentration camps.[33]

Today they had celebrated the restoration of their health and wealth, of their families and freedom. It was far more than a silver wedding anniversary, it was a celebration of life and it was greeting the future as children of God and as Australians, free to be. For the moment, at least, they were a big family, supporting and nurturing each other, having fun and working together, exploring opportunities and growing. They were building their church on the Margate Road, and had begun planning to build a school for their children like the schools they had attended, where parents accepted the responsibility of teaching their children. They had been faithful, they continued to be faithful, and God had blessed them, as he had blessed Job.[34]

■ ■ ■

ENDNOTES

1. FEESTPROGRAMMA ter gelegenheid van het SILVEREN HUWELIJKSFEEST van EERKE JACOB VAN DER LAAN en TONI AUGUSTE BANDHOLZ. Kingston, November 12, 1954. (Celebration program on the occasion of the silver wedding anniversary of Eerke Jacob van der Laan and Toni Auguste Bandholz), trans. Kees Wierenga. http://www.dutchtasmanianconnection.com/uploads/6/4/6/1/64611139/vdlaan_25th_wa.pdf.
2. K. Bolt, *Letters from Tasmania* (Bloomington, Indiana, USA: AuthorHouse, 2015), 20–29.
3. P. Laning, "Dagboek van Peter, Teddy, Tjark op Lampadusa 15 Juni 1943 tot 9 Juli 1943" (Diary of Peter, Teddy, Tjark on [the island of] Lampadusa June 15 to 9 July 9, 1943). Laning family papers, translator Kees Wierenga.
4. Bolt, *Letters from Tasmania*, 25.
5. Bolt, *Letters from Tasmania*, 81–88; ABC Letters, letter of March 11, 1950. The ABC letters were written in Dutch, mostly by Eerke van der Laan, also by Ep Pinkster, from 1950 to 1952 inclusive, to inform family, friends and acquaintances in the Netherlands of the purpose of the group that migrated to Kingston, and to report on the situation, needs and achievements in Tasmania. Trans. Kees Wierenga.
6. ABC Letters, letter of September 4, 1950.
7. Minutes of the Kingborough Municipal Council, February 11, 1952.
8. Interview with Colin Walton, son of the grocer, Mrs Walton, February 2018.
9. ABC Letters, letter of August 14, 1950.
10. ABC Letters, letter of January 28, 1952 and November 1, 1952.
11. O. M. Roe, *Life over Death: Tasmanians and Tuberculosis* (Hobart, Tas.: Tasmanian Historical Research Association, 1999): 126, 131, 140–144.
12. P. Laning, Invitation and covering letter dated September 1954. Copy held by Wierenga family.
13. Bolt, *Letters from Tasmania*, 19.
14. Bolt, *Letters from Tasmania*, 19
15. Bolt, *Letters from Tasmania*, 67–74.
16. Bolt, *Letters from Tasmania*, 11, 83.
17. Bolt, *Letters from Tasmania*, 18.
18. *The Mercury*, April 9, 1959, 19 and April 10, 1959, 29.
19. *The Australian Women's Weekly*, February 11, 1959.
20. Minutes of the Kingborough Municipal Council, July 15, 1957.
21. Interview with April van der Laan (née Taylor), November 2017.
22. R. Julian, *The Dutch in Tasmania: An Exploration of Ethnicity and Immigrant Adaptation*, (Tas.: University of Tasmania, March 1989), 124, 127.
23. R. van Zetten, *Getting Started: A Study of the Formative Years of the Reformed Churches of Australia: 1951–1957*, (Geelong, Vic.: Reformed Theological College, September 1988), 32–37.
24. Bolt, *Letters from Tasmania*, 42ff.

25. 2 Corinthians 12:8–10.
26. Eulogy http://www.dutchtasmanianconnection.com/folkerts-bart.html.
27. Reformed Church of Kingston, membership roll.
28. ABC Letters, letter of June 17, 1950.
29. ABC Letters, letter of June 22, 1950.
30. Bolt, *Letters from Tasmania*, 71.
31. Interview with his daughters, December 2007.
32. "Migrant Assimilation and Building Tasmania", Channel Museum exhibition, Margate, Tasmania; *The Mercury*, April 19, 1959, 19.
33. Bolt, *Letters from Tasmania*, 82.
34. Job 42:10–17.

PUBLICATION HISTORY

Four of the articles in this anthology have been previously published.

"How archaeology helped save the Franklin River"
Dr Billy Griffiths
Previously published in *The Conversation* (Friday Essay), March 2, 2018.

"The passing of the 'tigerman'"
Nic Haygarth
Partly published as a blog, George Wainwright/Brown/Wilson (1864–1903), Woolnorth "tigerman" nichaygarth.com, December 17, 2016.

"Constitution Dock: construction, naming and tragedies"
Terry Newman
Original version published EAST-V-WEST, *The Mercury*, September 15, 2001, 41–2.

"Job in Tasmania"
Kees Wierenga
http://www.dutchtasmanianconnection.com/migrant-documents.html, December 2018

www.ingramcontent.com/pod-product-compliance
Lightning Source LLC
Chambersburg PA
CBHW061138010526
44107CB00069B/2978